Do Cats Think

Notes of a cat-watcher

Paul Corey

CASTLE

This book is for my grandson
Alex David Mathews

Contents

Introduction

Did you ever wonder whether you have been missing a great opportunity in the way you relate to the cat you live with?

The trouble in dealing with pets is that, imbued as we are with the Judeo-Christian Ethic which places man in a special category, we often overlook the fact that the minds of other mammals work just the way ours do. And that the workings of all mammalian minds are limited by the frames of reference that have shaped them.

I have heard lots of people say that animals—meaning mammals other than man—do not think, or reason, or make decisions. Only man is supposed to have such capabilities. All other animals act simply from instincts and/or reflexes. They do not *think*, they *function*.

Reflexes? Yes. All mammals, including man, act reflexively in given situations. Instincts? No. "Instinct" is a word created by man to cover his ignorance of behavior.

Many times I have watched one of my cats sit in the yard and look around. From time to time its head will pause briefly in one position before moving on.

Sometimes these shifts in its gaze will be repeated. Then it will get up and set off in one of the directions that had occupied its attention.

Was this cat idly casting its glance around without even some faint activity going on in its cortex? Or had it been thinking: over there is a brush pile—rats, mice, ground squirrels; that way is a thicket—rabbits, quail, birds; that way live the neighbors and their snooty calico. Words don't form in this cat's mind, but images must—*something* to tie interest to what its eyes see. Where is the action? Where will be the best chance of getting food or having fun and excitement?

Then something clicks in its brain. It makes up its mind; it reaches a decision and takes off.

Is there any difference between its behavior and yours when you sit on your terrace or porch and wonder what you should do this afternoon? You look toward the garden shed: it needs tidying and reorganizing. You look down at the lawn: has it grown enough to require mowing? Perhaps you look up at the eaves of your house: should I check the troughs and clean out the leaves? Then, perhaps you just say "the hell with it, this is my day off," and stretch out for a nap.

I've seen my cats arrive at apparently the same decision and do the same thing.

My friends and acquaintances quite often express amazement when one of our cats shows that it remembers them. But that remembering is no big deal. Sometime, in that cat's frames of reference, this person had come on strong. We have to bear in mind that the cat's brain, any nonhuman brain, is not cluttered with the fantastic number of conflicting facts, incidents and abstractions that the human brain is. So it's much easier for odor, movements and voice sounds to trigger the memory of you in its brain than it is for such stimuli to bring memory to you of some person you met casually at a party a year ago.

Some people seem amazed that cats and other non-human animals play games and have fantasies. If you remind yourself of the limitations of their frames of reference, you will realize their behavior is no different from yours, except perhaps in degree.

We bought a horse for our daughter, Anne, when we came to California. The animal's name was Clipper and she was a feisty character who came from a ranch that had ten or a dozen horses. At our little place she found herself alone.

One cool June evening I went into the pasture to get her. She charged me, rearing on her hind legs and baring her teeth. I was scared. Was she vicious? I waved my arms and yelled, "Clipper!"

She brought her front feet down, trotted a little way off, then turned and looked at me. I read a strange expression in her eyes, a puzzled expression which I went on to interpret as embarrassment.

Was it?

On cool summer evenings a herd of horses often gallops and plays and has mock battles. That evening, Clipper was full of spirit and play. She was lonely. So perhaps she fantasied me as one of her horse friends and pretended to attack me.

Perhaps the expression in her eyes was not unlike one that has been in mine—and yours, too, on occasion—when I've directed a playful pass or friendly remark at someone I thought I knew walking ahead of me on the street, only to discover that he or she was a stranger.

I have a friend, Wendy Ramsay, who lives with an

affectionate cat named Josephine. Wendy has a habit of picking Josephine up, talking to her tenderly and kissing her on the end of the nose. Once, after such a kiss, Josephine put her mouth around the tip of Wendy's nose and bit it. The bite wasn't hard, but Wendy felt the points of sharp little teeth.

She dropped Josephine angrily and gave her a loud scolding. The cat's reaction was to show hurt feelings, badly hurt feelings. She wouldn't go near Wendy. She would sit on the floor on her brisket, back to Wendy, demonstrating indignation, disapproval and, perhaps, the feeling that she'd been very much misunderstood.

After Wendy got over her own indignation, she reviewed the incident. She had kissed Josephine on the end of the nose. A cat doesn't have a mouth like a human mouth. Perhaps Josephine, wanting to return the kiss, had come as near to it as her anatomy would permit by putting her mouth around the tip of Wendy's nose.

Acting upon this interpretation, Wendy relented and made up to Josephine. They became reconciled, and my friend resumed the nose-kissing routine. As soon as Josephine felt reassured she had been forgiven for what had been interpreted as an aggressive act, she again returned Wendy's kiss by putting her mouth around the tip of my friend's nose, but more gently. This little demonstration of affection has now become a regular thing between them.

For people who live with cats, the careful observation and understanding of their behavior can pay off in fascinating and gratifying revelations. Most of my life I have observed at close hand the fifteen cats we have lived with over the years. This book is about what the watching of these feline companions has revealed to me.

1

Cat-Watching
in the Cybernetic Age

There are all sorts of "watchers"—bird-watchers, people-watchers, star-watchers. "Watching" sometimes is a great pastime. But what, you ask, can cat-watching have to do with cybernetics, or the science of communication?

Let's take a look into the future. It is reasonable to assume that, before the year 2000, computers and automation will create an age when people will work only a few job-hours a week. What are we going to do with all the leisure time we will have?

In his article, "Time, Leisure and the Computer: The Crisis of Modern Technology," Dr. Glenn T. Seaborg, while still chairman of the U.S. Atomic Energy Commission, wrote that "it is a failure of imagination to believe that a transition to the Cybernetic Age cannot be made in which leisure can become central to man's existence and his greatest blessing." He called for "bold new concepts" to fill this future time-on-our-hands.

Fishing and philatelism may suffice for some. But a person with a creative turn of mind will want a time-occupier that is productive. This avocation can, and probably should, use the service of a computer, but it

should not be something that a machine can do better
than man and thus automate out of man's reach.

Such a "bold new concept" is suggested in the
book, *The Mind of the Dolphin*, by Dr. John Cun-
ningham Lilly. He has made a study of interspecies
communication, using as his subject the bottle-nosed
dolphin, an aquatic mammal. I don't wish to imply that
everyone hunting a leisure-filler should get his own
bottle-nosed dolphin. But I do feel that the subject selected should be some sort of mammal, not a bird or a
fish, because man is a mammal and that will put him
and his subject in the same ball park.

As Dr. Lilly found, a basic requirement is humil-
ity, plus respect for the other guy. No matter which
mammal you select to watch, you should be ready to
accept the fact that all mammals are animals and that
man, too, is an animal. Man may be technically farther
advanced, but there is considerable doubt that he has
advanced morally and ethically as far as many other
species.

Man's efforts to prove himself *not* an animal have
been going on ever since his first wanton murder. The
French philosopher Descartes pointed out that even
idiots can arrange words to make known their
thoughts, but "no animal can do the same." A cat can
make known his thoughts to anyone who understands
his language by the subtle movement of the tip of his
tail or the twitch of his whiskers. No human animal
can do that.

Mortimer Adler, who I'm sure thinks of himself as
a philosopher, wants, before he will abandon man's
nonanimal image, a zoologist to "discover a nonhuman
species of animal the members of which engage in conversation with one another." He doesn't specify
whether that conversation be carried on in English,

Latin or Hebrew, but I assume he expects it to be some human-animal language. This alone shows Mr. Adler's appalling ignorance of nonhuman animals and, maybe, of the human animal as well.

Once you have really accepted the fact you are an animal, you should select an animal partner for this watching game with which you are in rapport. No matter how seriously you take animal-watching as a leisure-time occupation in the Cybernetic Age, you may not improve interspecies communication. But you will discover interesting and enlightening things in your subject's behavior, and you just might hit upon something that will improve the human animal.

My wife Ruth and I, who have one daughter, have lived with fifteen cats: seven ginger tabbies, one with a crinkled ear; five Siamese; a black-and-white; and two with gray and black tabby patches on white, one of them a Manx. Most of this time we have been an integrated family: no separate-but-equal jive here. There's no "putting the cat out" at bedtime. All of those years we have been interested, even dedicated, cat-watchers. However, only recently have I come to realize the possibility of cat-watching as a new concept for productive leisure-time.

Carl Van Vechten in *The Tiger in the House* points out that St. George Mivart insisted that "the Cat rather than Man was at the summit of the animal kingdom and that he was best-fitted of mammalians to make his way in the world." You may disagree, but if you live with a cat or cats on terms of mutual acceptance and equality, you will soon understand why the cat has been deified in past cultures.

The cat, in dignity and independence, is very much like the human animal should be but isn't. Perhaps that's my strongest reason for choosing the cat as a subject for the human animal to watch: some of the cat's dignity and independence may rub off on the watcher.

To anyone suggesting "man's best friend," the dog, as a study-subject, I can only shrug. I would like to point out that if we eliminated the dog from our lives, nothing much would happen to our ecology. Independent of man, the dog is a vandal. With man, he does a little sheep-herding, a little watch-dogging. He helps law enforcement officers control troublesome ghetto-dwellers and protest marchers. He sniffs out "hash" and "grass." He goes out on weekends and helps man murder other forms of life for pleasure. But mostly he is just an adjunct to man's ego.

I don't dislike dogs: some of my best friends have been dogs. But dog-lovers are dog-lovers because they need something servile near them. They need a live thing that will show affection on command. Or, when job-boss-mate-kids-Life beat on them, they need something they can beat on in turn, something that will cringe and crawl and obey and show no resentment afterwards. They need something that will leave its daily "pile" for others to step in, thus visiting, by proxy, the vengeance of their immature characters upon the world around them.

A bitter summing up? Right. I intended it that way. The dog is too much like man is, rather than as he should be. I'll leave it to Frances and Richard Lockridge in their book *Cats and People*, probably the best book on *Felis domestica* ever written, to put the case for dogs more kindly: "Most dogs are unemployed," they say. "A dog does not live by working; he lives by charm, and has for generations."

A great many cats don't work, and many cats get a lot of mileage out of charm. But a healthy cat will always work (although I doubt he would consider it such) if he has the chance—and feels like it. He will never turn on charm at the snap of a finger—unless, of course, he happens to feel like being charming. In that event, the finger-snap is merely incidental.

The cat owes man nothing. Some experts estimate that there is one homeless cat managing on its own for every one with a home, which makes a total cat population in the U.S. of more than fifty million. That means the largest nonhuman animal population in the nation, short of rodents, whose number is beyond estimate. Eliminate cats from our ecology and, in a matter of weeks, we would be overrun by rodents.

Let's approach this cat-watching idea from another angle. *Time* magazine stated that Sherwood L. Washburn, a Berkeley, California, anthropologist, "has shown, for instance, that primate curiosity—which in Man would be called *basic research*—comes into play when the animal is well-fed and secure; only then is he in the mood to gratify this intellectual need."

Curiosity, or the urge to do "basic research," has always been a characteristic specifically attributed to the cat, only it is supposed to do *him* in. Perhaps this only happens to those cats who are not "well-fed and secure," and are forced to do their "basic research" on a more desperate basis. When man is forced into basic research in a hurried, desperate basis, he usually meets disaster, too.

Our own cats are well-fed and as secure as we can make them. They spend hours every day in the basic research of their world. They have definite chores and responsibilities.

I don't know if that is how they consider them. The younger cats have always learned their general behavior in the household from the older ones. From time to time, they create new routines and new codes of conduct of their own volition when situation and circumstance necessitate.

Ruth and I are free-lance writers. As such, it has been necessary to train ourselves to observe carefully what goes on around us. We have watched our cats, not as a leisure occupation, but because we have all lived together under the same roof. Most of the time we work at home and have been able to observe them. With the exception of a few months, we have lived in the country—Putnam County, New York, and Sonoma County, California—which has permitted our cats the widest possible natural freedom for their own lives.

During all my years of cat-watching, I wasn't looking for anything special. I was just observing the behavior of cats for my amusement.

I know my cat companions understand my language better than I understand theirs. Although their brains are smaller than mine, I can't help but interpret this achievement of theirs as a show of superior ability of some kind—a superior intelligence or sensitivity or something important to know more about. Intelligence in animals, including the human animal, is a relative thing. What goes on in a brain, any brain, is still a great mystery.

A psychologist we know has spent years trying to find out how the brain works. He uses cats for his tests because the cat's brain, he says, is most nearly like the human brain. Typical of such testing is one he made and reported while a special research fellow at California Institute of Technology. It dealt with "neural correlates of perceptual integration." He wrote: "To facilitate analysis, a brightness relation was used: the animal was given a food reward for selecting the brighter of two lighted panels." After repeated tests, a neurosurgeon removed part of the subject's brain and, following convalescence, the tests were repeated. The results should come as a surprise to no one: the subject, with the brain it had left, again "learned" to select the brighter panel to get its food reward.

Perhaps this finding is important. To me it seems obvious—and rough on the subject. It is an almost classic example of "scientific experimentation." The routine must be one that another scientist can duplicate and get the same results, even if the results are not of very much value.

The food-reward bit is routine research practice when testing nonhuman animals for intelligence, "learning ability" or, as in the above instance, to see how the brain works. A half-starved animal will "learn" a lot of routines to get food. Sometimes mild forms of pain are added to speed the process. But none of this can really be called "learning" except in the most elementary sense. It is simply a conditioning of basic reflexes, a mammal's reaction to hunger and fear.

Frantic hunger reduces cerebration to such elemental action that the results, rather than indicating intelligence or learning ability, reveal only how well a brain functions at its lowest level—at survival level. Go hungry for a couple of days, and then try to make out your income tax report.

Another example of the creative poverty in the accepted "scientific method" of testing is a recent experiment made by a rat psychologist. He separated litters of rats. One group was placed in an "advantaged" environment, while the other was placed in a "disadvantaged" environment. After a period, the rats were killed and their brains measured. The brains of the rats from the advantaged environment were larger than those from the disadvantaged environment.

Any welfare worker or observer of ghetto vs. nonghetto dwellers would probably arrive at a similar conclusion, without having to kill the subjects and measure their brains.

The psychologist we know freely admits the artificial limitations and unimaginative restrictions placed on the study of mental processes. As Richard H. Rube, a professor of materials science and electrical engineering at Stanford University, says, "One of the most pernicious falsehoods ever to be almost universally accepted is that the *scientific method* (italics are mine) is the only reliable way to truth."

However, because of the immense cost, both in money and in time, no qualified researcher can observe a nonhuman animal in its normal, free existence, carrying out its daily "basic research" in well-fed security, and screen out and evaluate its actions that might be interpreted as cerebration.

Dr. Lilly and his assistant Margaret Howe studied Peter Dolphin in this way. Their findings, although revealing, constitute only an isolated study.

Now, this is where the cat-watching, or any animal-watching, game fits into the Cybernetic Age. A hundred or a thousand people, with time on their hands and no special, expensive equipment, could observe and report on the day-to-day behavior of an animal in one species and produce a significant body of information on that animal's communication. Fifty accounts of cats, albeit different cats, whose actions might be correlated and interpreted as demonstrating ESP, for instance, might conceivably be accorded the status of ten repetitions of an ESP experiment under laboratory conditions. Such a suggestion will horrify qualified researchers; the interested leisure-time watchers will have to fight for recognition of the validity of their observations.

The trained scientific observer usually shrugs off the observations of the untrained. The lay observer will, on occasion, "read into" an action something that a more scientific mind might readily explain away.

But it is equally possible that the scientific explaining-away is based upon scientific ignorance, scientific misinformation or scientific bigotry. And it is naive to believe that the trained scientific researcher never shades his own reports from time to time if the renewal of a grant depends upon something spectacular to get the money coming again.

Fallibility is not limited to the nonscientific mind. Dr. Konrad Z. Lorenz, a Viennese naturalist widely recognized and approved by the scientific fraternity, includes a chapter called "Animals that Lie" in his book *Man Meets Dog.* He writes: "I shall show how wrong it is to think that the cat, the proudest and most upright of our domestic animals, is 'deceitful.' At the same time, I do not regard this inability to deceive as a sign of the cat's superiority. In fact, I regard it as a sign of the much higher intelligence of the dog that it is able to do so."

My first reaction upon reading this was shock that intelligence had been equated with deceitfulness. Is a liar more intelligent than an honest person? Perhaps so. If you accept that position, then perhaps it is right to assume that the more intelligent researcher will falsify his reports while only the stupid researcher will tell the truth.

I don't question Dr. Lorenz's assertion that the cat is "the proudest and most upright of our domestic animals." Why should I? I'm a cat-lover. But I do think it's a bit too extravagant.

However, to assert that a cat doesn't deceive shows an appalling lack of observation of cats, or of even one cat. A cat can hoodwink with the best of us. He can dissemble to get across a want. He can dissemble to play what I as a human animal consider a practical joke, or to get back at someone, human or nonhuman, for a trick played on him.

But I have never known a cat to dissemble to cover a weakness of his own, or to try to get something that wasn't in a sense rightfully his. Dr. Lorenz simply knows little about cats. He is a dog-lover. Yet, his pronouncements are accepted by "scientifically minded

readers" as valuable contributions to understanding
the living world; he has been awarded the Nobel Prize
in science.

Another fear expressed by established researchers
is that the nontrained observer's report will be clouded
by "anthropomorphism," or attributing human motives
or behavior to animals. That's a booby-trap word produced by man's assumption that man is not an animal.
The basic nervous system of all mammals is the same;
hence the reaction to like stimuli will be alike, or will
differ only to the extent of differing frames of reference. The new scientific field of biosociology studies
just these kinds of parallels, in fact—from a properly
remote, "scientific" distance.

Certain bits of anthropomorphism are bound to
creep into a report but needn't harm it. For instance,
Leo Quartus—fourth of our ginger tabbies—brought a
full-grown rabbit into our house one early morning. It
was alive and unharmed. These are facts. It was also
Easter morning. Our interpretation, only half-serious,
that he had brought the Easter Bunny for our small
daughter might be called anthropomorphic. Yet, it
doesn't detract from the report. However, we *had* been
talking to our daughter about the Easter Bunny the
previous afternoon in the presence of this cat.

Likewise, the large tears shed by Leo Secundus
when we visited him in the animal hospital were a fact.
Anthropomorphically, it was easy for us to feel that
after being away from us for a week, he was overjoyed
to see us and that his tears were shed for the same reason we were shedding our own. Accepting the similar-
ity of mammalian nervous systems, there might have
been nothing anthropomorphic about it: we may all
have been acting alike to similar stimuli.

Then there is the Siamese cat now living with us
who, when he was younger, insisted on a piece of ched-

dar cheese when we had a snack at bedtime. After eating it, he immediately went outdoors. That is a fact to satisfy any conscientious researcher. But I couldn't help it if Ruth anthropomorphized that he went out with "baited breath" to sit in front of a mouse hole. Perhaps his breath smelling of cheese did help: he was a damned good mouser.

Watching the way nonhuman animals behave is rewarding, even if the observations are never shared. However, once the scientific world rids itself of the straightjacket of the rat-psychologist approach to data, trained people can collaborate with the leisure-time watchers to the advantage of both. After all, professional astronomers work with and accept the findings of amateur astronomers. And amateurs have made some important discoveries.

Cat-watching, or any kind of animal-watching, can't be automated, but the data resulting can be fed into a computer where it can be correlated and assessed. With a little imagination, perhaps a real breakthrough can be made in communicating with our fellow animals. Such an achievement could prove valuable when that day comes, perhaps in the not-too-far-off future, that we meet with an extraterrestrial intelligence. In fact, the whole "bold new concept" of creative leisure might prove that the abundance of leisure granted us by the Cybernetic Age was really not enough, after all.

2

How I Became a Cat-Watcher

Any conditioned cat-hater can be won over by any cat who chooses to make the effort. Only an unregenerate ailurophobe can't be reached. I'd say he's really sick.

A person can become conditioned to dislike cats in many strange ways. I once knew a guy who claimed he disliked cats ever since an experience during World War II. He was a civilian flight instructor stationed in Michigan. He lived with friends, and every morning the friend's wife dangled a kitten by the scruff of its neck in his face to awaken him.

I could have hated the woman for that, but not the cat.

Some people have equally strange reasons for loving cats. A retired West Point colonel I met in Cold Spring, New York, a bachelor, had thirty cats. He had had sixty, so he claimed, but a neighbor had poisoned half of them. All his military life he had been accustomed to having his orders obeyed. In retirement, he wanted just the opposite. So he surrounded himself with cats and was happy.

One summer years ago I considered myself an unrepentant cat-hater. The previous winter Ruth and I had lived at Bandol-sur-Mer on the Riviera. The real estate agent who rented us our villa also provided us with a young female cat. Shortly after we got her, she had her first heat. She screamed her appeal for satisfaction, which seemed amusing for a while. She also developed a taste for French pastry and yowled around the villa for that. Both of her desires increased as the months passed: no tomcat put in an appearance, and our shortage of francs reduced the amount of pastry that came into the house.

Now, I can respect natural sex urges and I can applaud a taste for French pastry, but I'm damned if I could put up with all that screaming. Finally we gave her to a French shopkeeper, and I was determined never to have another cat.

A year later we were living in the country near the west end of Putnam County, New York. We had divided a twenty-five acre rocky, wood-and-scrub-covered piece of property with another couple. It lay at the end of a thousand-foot dirt track that ran up from the Albany Post Road.

In the split of the land, we took the smaller parcel which was closer to the highway. We lived in a small cottage on the dirt tract still closer to the Post Road. Our friends and co-buyers lived in a house on the main portion of the acreage.

That summer I roughed in another cottage on the lower portion of our eight acres. In late August another couple, friends of ours, came to vacation in that unfinished house. They had a black cat named Felix, a long, lean, handsome cat, if you fancy long lean cats.

Felix spent much of his time crying and complaining. That didn't bother me, because I wasn't living with him. But it confirmed my notion that cats were naggers, and that I wanted no such irritant around.

Our friends in this country-living venture wanted a cat. The wife wanted a female. To me that was crazy, but it was their problem. This area of New York State

was summer-home, New York City-commute country.
Some summer people offered our friends a pair of kittens. They were rufous, or ginger or orange-yellow,
and part Persian, a brother and sister. The sole stipula-
tion was that the two weren't to be separated, at least
not permanently separated. Brother and sister were to
be able to see each other occasionally.

The sister was taken by our friends. They figured
that if the owners of Felix took the brother, the kittens
could get to see each other down in the city. However,
the black cat had nothing but unfriendly remarks to
make to the young orange-yellow tom.

That was the situation on that last Sunday evening
in the unfinished cottage. Ruth and I dropped in with
several bottles of home brew for a final visit before the
couple returned to the city the next day. Our friends
who wanted to keep the sister were there, and the ginger tom, already named Leo, was in the cottage. Felix,
the black cat, was outside and wouldn't come in.

As soon as we arrived, the urging began for us to
take the tom. That would make an ideal arrangement:
brother and sister would then live close together in the
country for most of each year.

I promptly demurred. Cats could be a damned nuisance. Their persistent crying and complaining would
drive me nuts.

We continued to talk and drink home brew, and
the conversation got away from cats. It went on and on.
Some time during it the ginger tom climbed into my
lap, curled up and went to sleep.

Why did he pick me? There were five other laps
present, all of them more friendly than mine.

It's that sort of coincidental behavior of cats that
upsets people. It raises the question: did he know *I* was
the guy who had to be won over? But won over to what?
He couldn't possibly have understood all the talk that
had gone on about him and his sister. Or could he
have?

It's easy to say "Pooh, pooh! It just happened that way." I dare say that cat-lovers and cat-watchers can cite many similar instances. If these were computerized and studied and compared, some pattern just might be revealed. And perhaps a little better understanding of the mind of another mammal just might come through to the mighty genus *Homo*.

Of course, in this instance Leo's home still wasn't determined. Oh, no. I wasn't to be won over so easily. However, our friends who wanted to keep the sister— now called Penelope, already shortened to Penny— went back to their cabin, where she had been left shut in. If Leo stayed with the black cat's people there could be a real brawl. Felix's people wanted very much to keep the kitten but were unhappy about making Felix unhappy. So Ruth and I offered to take Leo home for the night. In the morning, we said, something could be worked out.

Ruth carried the flashlight and lighted the dirt road down to our cottage. I carried Leo. He didn't struggle to get away or get down, not even once. That's the way I remember it. He didn't cry or complain. He just purred a very large purr.

At home I spread out newspapers and put a shovel of dirt on them. Perhaps we offered him milk or food. Then we went to bed. I think he curled up on Ruth's bed, the lower in our double-decker setup. I think that once in the night I heard him use his dirt: in the morning it showed use. But there was never a complaint out of him.

By breakfast time, I had to admit that his presence had not caused a crisis. In the daylight I could see how beautiful he really was. He was chunky, or cobby; his face was wide and round, his nose short, his eyes golden, his ears short and tufted at the tips. A suggestion of tiger stripes marked his body. His tail was thick, not long, and with a distinct kink at the very end.

He drank milk, he used his dirt again, he played, he purred when we petted him. Occasionally he would open his mouth and give a very faint miaow. I thought he had a speech defect. I hadn't yet heard of the "silent miaow," or of its effectiveness. He simply couldn't miaow the way many cats can and do.

This meant that he never miaowed for food; he purred. He never miaowed to be let out; he made such desires known by scratching—gently—or by sitting patiently in front of the door or window.

That voice limitation set a pattern of cat miaowing with us for forty-five years. His son, Leo Secundus, although he had normal speech, picked up his father's quiet habit when he came to live with us. He in turn passed it on to his younger brother, Leo Tertius. And it has been handed down from cat to cat to the present.

But that September Monday the pressure built up: if we would just keep Leo—please—then the brother and sister wouldn't have to be returned to their former family. I had to admit that he had been in no way objectionable—so far.

What I didn't tell anyone at the time was that, when I was a three-year-old kid on a farm in Iowa, I had had a ginger kitten I called Butter. It was allowed in the house when I was sick that winter and I played with it. When I got well, it was returned to the barns from whence it came. And, like many farm cats, it disappeared. I had loved that kitten. It was perhaps the first thing in my life I was ever conscious of loving.

So, you see, the dice were really loaded in Leo's favor. We kept him another night. We pretended his future was still in the balance. But by the end of the week, I was hooked.

Once we decided to keep him, I was determined that he be properly disciplined. There was to be no permissiveness about his upbringing. We whistled when

we wanted him to come—no "kitty, kitty" nonsense. He
was spanked for getting on the eating table and told
loudly, "No!" and "Bad!" for any sort of mischief that
he as a young cat just naturally got into.

Most of the whacking became my chore. Afterwards, he'd go under the bed or to some other secure
place and make like a lion-on-the-library-steps with his
forepaws folded beneath his chin. To me he looked
hurt, miserable and thoughtful. Anthropomorphically
speaking, maybe he was considering his folly in win-
ning me over. And who can say he wasn't? After letting
him "think" for a while, I got down on the floor and
talked to him. I told him I wasn't mad at him. I explained over and over to him just why he had been
spanked and that he mustn't repeat what he had done
or he would get spanked again. I talked and explained
and coaxed until finally he came out of his sanctuary,
purred and forgave me.

To any human observing, I must have looked and
sounded pretty weird. Perhaps that's how Leo saw it.
But by the end of September, when we were ready to
move to a small apartment in New York City, he had
become a responsible member of our family. Oh, he
still had kitten tricks. He still got into mischief, some
of which went too far and for which he got spanked.
And he still let me coax him from sanctuary so we
could become friends again.

We bought a black cat carrier for the train ride to
the city. I worried that he would be frightened by the
trip and cause a scene. I worried that we might have to
check him in the baggage car and that he'd be terrified.

Once on board, we placed the carrier on the floor
under the edge of the seat and waited for the conductor
to come along and punch our tickets. From time to
time, one or the other of us would put our fingers down
to the screen of the carrier and let him sniff them for

reassurance. When the conductor-danger had passed, we lifted the box to the seat between us. Leo sat on his brisket, front paws folded, looking out the screen-covered opening. When we looked at him, he'd open his mouth, as was his habit, but no sound came out. He did not seem afraid.

We took a taxi from the station to our apartment. The landlady had told us we could keep a cat if he was clean. Leo was clean enough in the country. But life in a strange, cooped-up place in the city without trees, grass, or honest dirt could be quite a different thing.

In the apartment we let him out of his carrier and he inspected the place, as all cats do. There wasn't much to inspect: a large room with a daybed, a kitchenette and a semi-bath. I tore up part of the Sunday paper and put it in a pan at the end of the bathtub. He inspected what I did, and I tried to indicate that this was his privy by scratching a hole in the shredded paper with my fingers. He probably thought I was playing a game.

That night he slept between us on the bed. Perhaps he got up in the night and prowled around—I don't remember. I'm sure he ate in the morning and drank milk, but he did not use his pan. No doubt I showed it to him a number of times and explained its purpose, and he probably inspected it at my behest, but he didn't use it.

Ruth went to her job and I went looking for one. I got home earlier than she did, and Leo's pan was still untouched.

We ate dinner. He might have eaten something. I don't remember specifically anything that he did. It was what he *didn't* do that bothered me.

He had been holding everything for more than twenty-four hours. He must have been suffering.

By nine o'clock, I was suffering with him. We showed him his pan repeatedly. We scratched in the scraps of paper and sat him over the spot. We tried all manner of communication. We let the water trickle in the tub. We went "sssssss."

It seemed incredible he could hold out so long.

Ten o'clock came and I couldn't take any more of it. I got a paper bag, went over to Central Park, and scooped it full of dirt from amongst the shrubbery. Back in the apartment, I spread some of it over the shredded paper in the pan. Leo accepted that. He made his own hole, sat over it and damned near flooded the place. He was relieved and so were we.

We should have known enough to get dirt from the park earlier, or we should have brought some down from the country with us to help him adjust to apartment living. But people we knew who had cats in the city used pans with shredded newspapers for privies. Of course, most of those cats had started out as kittens with shredded-newspaper privies. That was before the days of commercial kitty litter. And it didn't occur to us that there might be a problem for a cat raised to use dirt.

That winter we learned much about Leo and, perhaps, about cats in general. He still had a lot of kitten in him, and our small apartment offered little to make up for his freedom in the country. He made friends with the landlady and chased the floor mop when she tidied up the apartment. But that could only distract him for a few minutes, and there was the rest of the day—until we got home.

So, come evening, we very often found Ruth's powder puff on the floor, having been well played with. If she carefully put it away in the dresser drawer, he would find some other item from the dresser top to play with. He had been taught to stay off such furniture, but here he was, obviously breaking such training when our backs were turned.

The usual judgment would be: that's a cat for you. We couldn't discipline him during the day, but at night, if he so much as made a move toward the dresser top, he got scolded and sometimes spanked.

One morning, I was writing letters and he was amusing himself with one of his toys. Suddenly he stopped, stared intently up at the dresser and crouched to spring. I yelled at him and he took sanctuary. It was the direction of his look that had caught my attention. I got down on the floor where he had been, looked up at the dresser and straight into my reflection in the mirror. He had suddenly seen another cat to play with— perhaps, in his mind, his sister Penny. Who knows?

From that time on, I made a point of tilting the mirror so that the reflection didn't strike the floor when we left the apartment. Small items on the dresser top were undisturbed. Sometime later, Ruth mentioned that Leo hadn't stolen anything from the dresser lately. The next morning I shifted the mirror, directing the angle of reflection to the floor. When I got home in the afternoon, the powder puff was on the rug. All of which only proved that Leo's reactions were hardly different from human reactions when bored. As with many human animals, boredom led to mischief.

Our apartment windows opened onto a flat roof. To let Leo get some air, we occasionally permitted him to go out on this roof. This was New York, and he got dirtier than he was able to handle. So we gave him a bath in the tub. He let us without much protest, but when we took him out to dry him and he saw his usually fluffy tail looking tight and bedraggled, his face filled with shame and humiliation and he ran and hid.

I'm sure words like *shame* and *humiliation* are anthropomorphic. But he had the same look on his face I've seen on a man's face when caught in a crowd with his fly open.

In the winter, no sunlight got into that apartment. But at night, when our lights were out, the light in an apartment across the court shone through the window and made a bright spot on the rug. I had insomnia and many nights I saw Leo curled up in that patch of light. When the people across the way turned out his "sun," he came to bed with us. His obvious longing for sunshine made me miserable, but the only thing we could do about it was to take him with us to the country on weekends.

One such weekend Leo spiked another of those behavioral myths people like to keep alive about cats. A favorite Sunday dinner of ours was meatloaf. Leo was most fond of meatloaf. On this particular Sunday, we ate early and went for a walk before getting ready to return to the city. The leftover meatloaf was left on the table to cool. To make sure Leo would be around when we got ready to go to the station, we left him in the cottage.

Two hours later, we returned to find him on the bench by the table, just below the meatloaf, paws folded beneath his chin. He hadn't touched the meat.

I have no explanation for his conduct. It contradicts the image most people have of cats, an image that, all too often, is quite true. He had been taught not to get on eating tables or any place where food was prepared. And he had apparently not forgotten that conditioning in the face of this stimulus.

We were shocked by the temptation we had placed before him. And I can assure you that he earned a sizable chunk of that meatloaf, fed to him in a dish on the floor where he usually ate. We also told him over and over that he was a very good cat.

I wouldn't have believed it possible at the time, but Leo passed this integrity on to his son Leo Secundus when he came to live with us. And each of our cats has picked it up from the older cats down the years.

Once, that winter in the apartment, we noticed that Leo wasn't eating. He didn't seem ill; no hot nose or dull fur. After a day, we began to worry. Then, one evening while we were reading, we heard a commotion in the kitchenette and he came forth with a mouse. He began playing with it while it was still alive. I killed it with my slipper. Then he ate it. After that he went to his food dish, polished off all the food in it and asked for more. We fed him more and praised him loudly for his mouse-catching.

Most people are horrified by cats' playing with live mice. It certainly isn't a pleasant sight. But over my years of cat-watching, I have come to realize that a young cat plays with a live mouse because he hasn't yet learned how to kill it. The mother cat brings in the live mouse to teach the kitten how to hunt and catch. And the poor mouse is usually worried to death unless someone else steps in and kills it.

This training routine with cat mothers is much like human parents' giving their children kittens to play with so that they will learn about animals. Very often that can be just as unpleasant to watch.

That fall Leo removed my last reservation about cats—about one cat, at least. Ruth had her job. I was trying to find one. It was the Depression, and the unemployed were selling apples on street corners. I was also trying to sell my stories, and the rejection slips piled up.

One afternoon I got home early and found several rejections in the mail. It had been a bad day of street tramping and no job encouragement, and I felt very sorry for myself. Alone in that cheap little apartment with no need for a stiff upper lip, I let go and blubbered like a hurt kid. Leo stared at me round-eyed. Then he climbed into my lap, sniffed my nose, and licked my cheek.

Sure, he may just have wondered about this weird keening sound I was making and liked the taste of salt in my tears. But, at the time, I preferred to believe he was somehow trying to console me.

3

Total Involvement

We didn't have Leo Primus neutered. The following summer, he mated with his sister Penny and she produced three kittens, two males and a female. One of the males was a light cream-yellow. We took him into our family and he became known as Leo Secundus, or "Sec."

The following spring, Leo mated with Penny again. Not long after, he was killed on the Albany Post Road, just a little more than a quarter of a mile from our cottage in the woods.

Now Sec was our Number One cat. Even before he was a year old, he showed a propensity for being a hard-luck cat. He had learned his conduct about the home from his father: don't cry for food; don't get on tables where food is prepared; don't get on the eating table ever—well, hardly ever.

The living room in our cottage started out as a porch. I glassed it in, and it was so pleasant that we ate there, wrote there in the daytime, and read there at night beneath an oil lamp. A pot-bellied stove stood near the kitchen door. The dining table faced the glassed-in wall overlooking a swampy area in the center. And at the far end was my desk, a couch, the most comfortable chair we owned, and a large trunk topped with a file box where the lamp stood in the evening. At this end we built a ladder to a casement window where we let the cats in and out. They didn't, at this time, have their own door.

Only eight feet wide and twenty feet long, you realize this room was rather crowded with furniture. And when our three chairs were pushed under the table, a forest of legs filled that area.

It was with this dining table that the first of many bad experiences happened to Sec. As I said before, he knew he shouldn't get on it. Why he did this time, I don't know. (You *know* you shouldn't run a red light, but you have.) It was possible he just wanted to see something that was going on out in the woods at that side of the house and the tabletop seemed the best vantage spot. Anyhow, the impulse was stronger at the moment than was his conditioning.

When I came in that afternoon, he was on the table. By the time I appeared, he realized his breach of conduct and scrambled off. In his dash beneath, he banged his nose on a table or a chair leg. It began to bleed.

I realized he had hurt himself and coaxed him out from his place of sanctuary. But there was no way to stop his nose from bleeding. A human animal in most such instances will breathe through the mouth. However, Sec insisted on breathing through his nose. After a while the blood would stop it up. To clear the passage, he would sneeze, which aggravated and prolonged the bleeding.

It was twenty-four hours before his nosebleed stopped and the proper breathing restored.

We didn't have Sec neutered, either, and by his second September he began to roam, as tomcats will. He strayed farther and farther from home and stayed away longer. We worried each time he was gone for more than a day, and rejoiced when he returned. He was, as I said, a hard-luck cat.

One weekend he didn't come back. I drove along the Post Road to see if he'd been hit. No sign of him. We told ourselves he'd show up later. After all, Leo had stayed away longer and still returned. But finally Leo hadn't come back. We worried.

Monday morning, for some reason, I went down to a patch of hazel brush and birch trees at the end of our chicken run. As I approached, I heard Sec's cry, unusually loud and demanding and downright desperate.

He lay in a corner of the brush. When he saw me, he pulled himself around with his front feet. I realized his hindquarters were paralyzed.

I couldn't tell what had happened to him or how he'd got there. The pads of his front paws were abraded, and his claws were worn as if he'd dragged himself a long distance. Perhaps his back had been broken by a blow. Maybe he'd been hit by a car.

I called Ruth, and we lifted him into a box. She held him on her lap the twenty miles to the nearest veterinarian. Sec didn't seem in pain, just unable to move his rear end. The vet examined him and determined that his back wasn't broken but that severe constipation had caused the paralysis. He thought he could fix him up, but we would have to leave him in his hospital.

We were distressed and considered having him put to sleep. After all, money was mighty scarce. We were free-lance writers and were not doing too well, despite Ruth's part-time job. Finally, we decided to let the vet try to bring Sec around.

All the way home we felt miserable. Sure, we had patted Sec's head and had said all sorts of comforting things to him. But what had gone on in his brain?

I remember his eyes, large and round, watching us as we left. Was he thinking anything like human thoughts? We could assure ourselves that the vet would treat him kindly, but how could we assure Sec? We could say to ourselves, "We've done the best we can for him. After all, he's only an animal."

Those are awfully empty words.

Over the years, I have come to feel that a mature cat, as Sec was, has the mentality of a three- or four-year-old child. But you can reassure children; you can tell them what's happening or going to happen. Can you get such reassurance across to a cat?

I suppose it is that sort of anthropomorphism that bugs the hell out of researchers whose job is to experiment on nonhuman animals. If they permit themselves such a comparison, they might not sleep well at night.

Later that week, I called the vet to find out how Sec was. He reported that he'd got his bowels functioning. He was still trying to restore some sort of life to the hind legs and would have to keep him in the hospital a little longer.

The following Monday we visited him, arriving early while the vet was still at breakfast. His assistant had opened the hospital and was feeding the patients. We saw cages of dogs and cats but no Sec. We called his name. Instantly we heard his loud, desperate cry. We hurried through the main section of the hospital and found him in the cardboard box we'd brought him in. It was on the floor in a separate wing of the building.

He pushed himself up with his front legs when he saw us. His eyes were round and frantic-looking. I dropped to my knees by the box and he pulled himself over the edge and into my lap. Huge tears formed in his eyes and ran down his cheeks.

Maybe they weren't tears of emotion at all. It was a chilly September morning. He had heard familiar voices. That had excited him. Excitement brings blood rushing to the head. The sudden blood heat

meeting the cold air on the surface had made his tear-ducts water. As simple as that.

And were the tears running down my cheeks caused the same way?

A lost child found by its parents couldn't have shown more feeling than Sec did upon seeing us again. Call my interpretation anthropomorphic, if you wish. It isn't possible to set up a like situation and check and recheck it in a test laboratory with proper controls. But does that prove my report less valid?

A brain is a brain is a brain. Simple basic reactions must be the same, no matter what the difference in skeletal structure of the mammal that houses it. I see no reason to doubt that Sec's feelings, within his frames of reference, were any different than yours or mine in a similar situation.

Of course, to feel that Sec understood we really hadn't abandoned him only made tougher for me what happened later—a couple of years later.

On this first visit, we found Sec actually looking much worse than he had when we'd left him there a week earlier. His back had been shaved from his shoulders to halfway up his tail. The vet explained that, to revive his hindquarters, he had had to apply a strong stimulant to the spine. He had painted the shaved area with Spanish fly, and the skin now was raw and blistered.

That seemed to me a strange method of treatment. I had always considered Spanish fly to be one of those myths talked about in bull-sessions. However, the dictionary says the Spanish fly is a green blister beetle and the source of *cantharides*, which is used externally as a *rubefacient* and a *vascatory*, and internally as a stimulant. (A *rubefacient* produces redness of the skin and a *vascatory* produces blisters.)

Anyhow, either the Spanish fly or just the natural

course of things had begun to show results. Sec could move his hind legs ever so slightly, proving that complete recovery might be possible. The vet wanted to keep him there a bit longer.

When we left, we told Sec he'd have to stay until the vet made him "all better." We told him to be a good cat and that we'd visit him again. We offered all the reassuring words one uses with a child in a similar situation.

Silly? A cat only hears and knows sounds and inflections. A cat doesn't know words and word meanings. Or does he?

He appeared happy to see us when we returned a week later, crying out at the sound of our voices. He purred loudly. He remembered us. Again he seemed to understand that we hadn't abandoned him.

Actually, he behaved like a mature human meeting a similar situation and adjusting to it. His condition gradually improved. Strength returned to his hind legs. He wasn't confined to a cage but was allowed to flop and wobble around the hospital. This freedom stimulated his recovery. He made friends with other patients. He stole dog biscuits. He "helped" the young assistant with his chores. "He's a character," the assistant told us. "We'll miss him when he leaves."

We visited him twice more before the vet felt he had recovered enough to go home.

Sec had been in the hospital thirty days. The bill was ten dollars. It was all we could afford and more than he, as an animal, was worth in the eyes of most human animals. But it did not approach a fair compensation for the vet's time and hospital treatment.

That vet was a man of real compassion. I've known two other vets, both specialists with small animals, and they too seemed to have more genuine feelings than most other humans.

Sec was far from recovered when we brought him home. He flopped from side to side when he tried to get

around. He had no control over his bowels. We had to
paint his back with a tarry ointment to keep the flies
off his raw, blistered skin and give it a chance to heal.
Having a sick animal around the house can be a messy
affair. More than once we wondered if we hadn't been
wrong in letting the vet save him instead of putting
him to sleep.

But Sec didn't like his condition any better than
we did. He looked terribly ashamed when he couldn't
control himself. However, being home where it was
warm did a lot for him. In only a day or two, he was
able to wobble to the door and go out when he needed
to. One of us always accompanied him. Ruth recalls
how he would look up at her with an expression like
gratitude when she steadied his hindquarters. But
there was a look of misery, too. A healthy cat's toilet is
an extremely private affair.

By the following March, he was well enough to
start roaming again. And we worried. One morning, he
came limping home with a crushed front paw and a
two-inch-long strip of skin pinched off. He had probably escaped the full bite of a steel trap's jaws and had
been able to pull free.

There didn't seem to be much a vet could do for
him that we couldn't do. I held him on my lap while
Ruth washed the wound. By that time his foot, I suspect, was fairly numb. Ruth was gentle with it and he
made very little fuss. He watched all she did.

Humans have the notion that some sort of antiseptic is as necessary on an animal's wound as on a person's. But "licking one's wounds" is not just a figure of
speech. If an animal can get at a wound, he can usually
keep it clean.

We behaved true to human form. However, we felt
that iodine would sting too much, so we settled for
Mercurochrome. When Ruth painted the wound and
the bright red of the medicine began to spread, he

didn't struggle. His leg trembled a little. But he hid his head in the open front of my sweater so that he couldn't see the effect. Every time she applied the antiseptic, he hid his eyes.

We have no explanation for his behavior. Maybe he didn't like the looks of the red stuff. However, some scientists maintain that cats, and all animals except humans, are color-blind. Maybe. Perhaps he merely thought that if he didn't watch what was happening, all of it would go away.

Our supposition that Sec had been injured by a steel trap was confirmed a few days later. I was holding him on my lap while Ruth tended his wound. She threw the cloth she had washed it with into the pot-bellied stove, and its door closed with a sharp, metallic snap. Sec shot off my lap and streaked under the couch. His action was pure reflex—a violently conditioned reflex.

As a kid in Iowa, I had used steel traps. I knew full well the sound of trap jaws closing.

I might have checked this deduction to a rat psychologist's satisfaction by getting such a trap and snapping it, perhaps out of his sight, and recording his reactions. I didn't need to.

I did go through the woods looking for traps, but I found none. A boy staying at a neighbor's was suspected of doing some trapping, but he didn't admit that Sec might have been injured by one of his.

Sec's injury kept him home that spring, hobbling around on three legs until his foot healed. It was always slightly clubbed after that. After recovering, he very often behaved in the way Dr. Lorenz says only dogs are capable of behaving.

All we had to do was to talk to him with a sympathetic tone and he would begin limping. Or he might be walking quite normally, but if he saw one of us he would begin to limp again.

Summer came and he resumed roaming. Again we worried. We considered that he was now too old to be neutered. Also, I was still hung up on having that done to a cat. Then, one Sunday morning in September, he didn't show up for breakfast. We said, "He'll be in later." Noon came and he hadn't appeared. Ruth called and whistled for him. No Sec. That afternoon she visited the neighbors to inquire if they had seen him. They hadn't.

Where should we look for him? Post Road? Not yet.

Before dusk, we took a walk up the hill at the north end of our land. It was thick with underbrush beneath tall oaks. From time to time, as we climbed, we called Sec's name or whistled. It seemed foolish and futile. What would he be doing up here? This was no place to hunt, and there were no traps at this time of the year. Maybe we should have chosen the Post Road.

We had climbed a hundred yards into the woods when he answered us. At first we weren't sure. There was a lot of Sunday traffic on the highway. But when we called again, his reply was unmistakable—eager, anxious and very strong.

Every time we called now, he answered and we moved toward the sound. But ahead in the brush we could see nothing. It was dogwood and the tops reached above our heads, closing in at the spot where we felt he had to be. Then we realized he was high up in a tree.

The young oaks were tall here, reaching for the sun. The slender trunks had no branches for at least thirty feet. We concluded that Sec had been treed by a dog and couldn't make it back down because of his previous injuries to spine and foot. Of course, once up the tree, above the undergrowth near the ground, he couldn't see when his enemy had gone away. For all he knew, it might still be there. After all, the underbrush was dogwood. Remember? We laughed about that later.

We called and coaxed, but he wouldn't even make a try to come down the branchless trunk. Finally, I climbed up to him, put him on my shoulder and slid back down. Thirty feet of oak tree eight or ten inches in diameter is not easy to shinny up and down. Sec grimly hung onto me. Besides the abrasions on my arms and legs, I had some fine claw marks on my shoulders. Safely down, I set him on the ground and we started home.

All the way to the house he stayed close to us. If he got a little ahead, he'd stop and look back. The expression in his golden eyes certainly wasn't fear or anger, or indifference or blankness. It struck me more like admiration or affection or respect. Certainly it was friendly.

But whatever his feelings, they seemed to make him self-conscious. As if to hide them, he would play a little, prance or wrestle a bunch of foxgrass in his clumsy way. We were very glad to have found him and felt he was glad, too, and showed it.

All that winter Sec came and went. Sometimes he would be away for a day or so and we would worry. He would return and we would relax. Then, in early March, he didn't come back. By the second day we were out searching for him, circling the neighborhood farther and farther. We drove up and down the Post Road looking; we walked the sides of the road searching the ditches to see if he had been only hit and had struggled away to die.

We talked to neighbors and people along the road. No one had seen him, or so they said. He had disappeared completely.

Day after day I would be working at my desk in the morning, or at some outdoor task in the afternoon, and I would pause and look around at the woods and fields. Suddenly my imagination would convince my eyes that I saw a spot of cream-yellow, and I would take off to check it out. I would find nothing. Or I would think, "Over there is a spot I haven't checked." And I would go check it. Or I would think, "Maybe I didn't check that area carefully enough." And I would go over it once more.

We never saw Leo Secundus again.

It was at least six weeks before the ache in my chest eased. Such feelings are probably ridiculous. After all, he was only a cat.

But I remembered his cries when I found him in the triangle with his back injured. I remembered his tears that first time we visited him in the hospital. I remembered his cries when we found him up the tree. And I could not keep from thinking, "Is he somewhere, trapped, injured, waiting for me to rescue him, and I'm not coming?" What went through his mind when I did not come?

I loved that hard-luck cat and I would not have let him down if I could have helped it. I had become totally involved in a cat's life, a committed cat-watcher.

Ten years later I learned what had happened to him.

On the other side of the Post Road from where we lived was a public garage and tearoom run by a couple, he of German descent, she of Irish. I seldom had occasion to go into the place. I don't remember why I was in there at this particular time. No more do I remember why they told the story in my presence. Maybe my presence pulled it out of their unconscious without their being aware of it.

But they told, each supplying details, how they once had caught a big, light yellow tomcat in a trap. It was many years ago—maybe ten years. And that big tomcat had attacked the man savagely, and the man shot him. Then the couple grew suddenly quiet.

Perhaps another memory disturbed them at that

moment. Ten years before I had stopped in and asked them if they had seen a big, light yellow cat. They said they hadn't. I remember the old woman next door, related to them by marriage, to whom I'd put the same question. She had said something about this couple and a cat. Then she grew silent and sullen.

Anyhow, maybe Leo Secundus hadn't suffered too much. Maybe he hadn't thought of me or waited for me to rescue him again. First came the pain of the trap jaws crushing him again. Perhaps he screamed at the hurt of it. Then he dashed here and there, pulling, struggling to escape. Finally the steel grip deadened the feeling in his foot. His efforts to free himself increased. He heard a stranger coming. He feared strangers. Fear. Struggle. Panic. Shock. Then had come the swift smashing of the bullet in his brain.

I hope he did not think I had let him down.

All this I remembered when I read Gavin Maxwell's story of the disappearance of his pet otter, Mij, in his book *Ring of Bright Water*. The animal, known to all the people where Maxwell lived, friendly with all people, had been clubbed to death by one of those people for its pelt.

Maxwell had searched the area calling to his pet for weeks, and the people who knew what had happened said nothing. Finally, one of them, graced a little more with what we like to think of as humanity than the others, told him. He said, "I couldn't think of you looking and calling for your pet up and down the burn and by the tide every day, and him dead all the while."

Reading that, I thought of Sec. There were people who knew of his death, but none had come forward to ease our weeks of torture. He was only a cat, and cats, according to some, are evil and torture the things they catch.

4

The Neutered Cat

Perhaps I overreact in my feelings of involvement with animals—cats especially. But over the years I have come to believe that when I take an animal into my home, my environment, I automatically assume full responsibility for it.

As Doris Day said, "People have Funds and Foundations and the Salvation Army, but animals have nobody."

That isn't quite true. There are many animal protection organizations run by good, conscientious, hardworking people. But basic responsibility rests with the person or persons who take animals into their lives. It is completely up to such persons to determine what is best for the health, happiness and safety of these animals, and to take the necessary steps to fulfill such requirements.

That's the general picture. As a cat-lover, I am stating the case for the cats.

To have your cat neutered, which means to have the males castrated and the females spayed, is not an easy decision to arrive at and accept. It is easier to entertain a philosophy that says your cat should remain "whole" and not be neutered. This is especially true should you and your cat be living in a small town or the country.

I've been through all that. Years ago, we took a sort of pride in the roamings of our first Leo. His home-comings were almost as good as a barometer. A day-time return meant a storm coming. If at night he jumped to the ledge of our bedroom window and wanted in, we would soon hear it raining, or awaken in the morning to find the ground covered with snow. He ate and slept until the weather improved and then re-turned to his roamings.

We gloried in his reputation as a fighter. No other toms ventured into his territory and stayed. Yet, he never came home clawed or with chewed and torn ears. Either he was so fierce or the competition so weak that he barely got scratched.

By the second spring, orange-yellow tabby kittens began appearing in litters throughout the neighbor-hood. To this day, we're told, his progeny still flourish in one section of that county.

Still, he was barely four years old, just entering the prime of his life, when he was killed. His death forced us to face the fact that had he been neutered he might have lived many years longer. In a sense, we had allowed him to go to his death.

By that time, his son Leo Secundus was too old to be neutered. That's what we felt at the time. He really wasn't, but the castration of a cat after he is a year old produces a different personality than castration be-tween the ages of six to ten months.

So we didn't have him neutered. But at that time we had taken another of Penny's kittens. He was from the last litter sired by Leo, a somewhat darker orange-yellow tabby than Sec. We faced up to the decision that we must have him neutered because we couldn't again handle what we had gone through with Leo and were going through with Sec.

This kitten became Leo Tertius, or "Tersh."

It was an extremely traumatic experience for me when the time came for us to take him to the vet and have him castrated. It is still, even today, a traumatic experience for me when that operation has to be performed on one of my cats. Much worse for me is the spaying of one of our female cats. But I have faced up to the necessity and accepted it. Or, perhaps I should say, I have rationalized it "for the cat's own good."

That is quite true. There is a long tradition in the world of the emasculation of animals, even the human animal. But years ago I did not know the kind of delightful change this operation would work on the personality of my cats.

There still is a lot of opposition to neutering, especially when the cat happens to live where it has a certain amount of freedom to roam. Much of the opposition is emotional.

With men a tomcat is a sort of projection of his own maleness, or machismo. A man can get vicarious pleasure from his tomcatting tomcat. I have known some men to refuse to have their tomcats neutered because their wives have been castrating them for years, and their cats become their last vestige of masculinity.

Women often reason that an unspayed cat is a way to teach the facts of life to their children. That's what they say. Actually, it all boils down to a type of voyeurism, with more interest in breeding and birthing than any true interest in children or cats.

The wife of someone we know refused to have their female cat spayed because, she said, "I want my children to watch the miracle of birth." When too many kittens accumulated, her husband took them up to the top of a mountain road near us and abandoned them in the brush.

We knew a grade school teacher who had cats. She had been married once and divorced. She claimed to

love cats. She kept no male cats and never had her female cats spayed. Every spring she announced to her
classes that she had kittens that needed homes. All a
youngster had to do to get a passing grade was to accept a kitten. The teacher never checked up to make
sure that kitten got a good home.

Not too long ago, a letter appeared in the local
paper, reporting that "Most of these heartless people at
least do their dirty work themselves, but today a
woman drove down our road in her big shiny new car
and made her child, who couldn't have been more than
five, throw two poor little kittens over the fence into
the field!"

Although I'm all for planned cat parenthood, there
is a lot for the cat-watcher to observe in the family life
of cats. It was September when Penny was about to
have her first litter of kittens and her people were
planning their return to the city. Ruth and I with Leo
were living in the cottage I had built back in the
woods. Mutual friends had moved into our first house
and planned to stay up in the country all winter, as did
we. So they offered to keep Penny and let her have her
kittens in the country instead of having to combine the
change to city life with the new experience of giving
birth.

As soon as her first three kittens were old enough,
Penny took them outdoors. "Kittengarden" was in ses-
sion. Penny dug a hole in the softest dirt she could find
and squatted over it. She sniffed the results, let the kittens sniff, then covered it carefully and elaborately.
These see-and-do lessons were repeated for several
days.

Some people will call her lessons "instinct." But to
me that word is a coverup for ignorance and the inability to find out, or a desire to find out, what really
happens.

Sometimes one of the kittens would squat over a hole Penny had dug, imitating her. If the kitten accomplished anything, Penny covered it and licked the kitten's cheek. If one of the kittens pretended this was a game, it got soundly cuffed. In a very short time all three kittens were completely trained.

Soon Penny began bringing them live mice "toys"—to catch, kill and eat. There were lessons in tree climbing, especially in coming down after once climbing up.

Penny was an exceptionally intelligent mother cat. I've known many not half as smart. And I've known neutered toms who were as smart or smarter as "mothers." But Penny was a mature cat when she had her first kittens.

Because cats like to be clean, the mother cats keep their kittens and the nest clean. As the kittens grow older, what the old cat has to clean up must certainly become disagreeable. Perhaps her brain puts things together: you take your wastes outdoors or into a sand box; if you take your offspring to the outdoors or the sand box, you'll be relieved of that disagreeable chore.

And the teaching of young cats by old cats goes on and on. A friend of ours here in California took in a very pregnant cat. After the kittens were born and given their early training, the mother cat took them out to the nearby field and taught them how to catch gophers. When she found fresh gopher workings, she waited in the grass, crouching, until the rodent pushed up a load of dirt. The kittens imitated her pose.

Like a small underground bulldozer, a gopher rolls a wave of freshly dug earth ahead of his front paws, chest and nose. He comes just far enough out of his hole that he can see around. Gophering cats remain motionless, intent. The rodent misled into believing all is safe, gives this load of dirt a sudden violent thrust forward.

In that movement, he is all the way out of his burrow. Not until that moment does the skilled cat pounce, hooking the little brown creature out upon the grass before he can escape back down his tunnel.

All of those kittens became great gopher hunters.

A sort of family life existed between Penny, the kittens and Leo. He visited them regularly when he was home. He never indicated in any way a threat to kill the kittens, as myth says tomcats are supposed to.

Penny was proud of their family, as any good mother cat is. She welcomed Leo, arching and rubbing against him, and seemed to appreciate his interest in their kittens. And he always behaved a bit aloof—after all, being a father was a new thing to him. But he let the kittens play with his tail and pretended not to notice. However, he never caught any mice for them, so far as we know, or helped with the early toilet clean-up and training.

Cats' fare in our neighborhood was milk, bread-and-milk, table scraps and breakfast food, especially oatmeal in the mornings. We believed that cats should eat what we ate. They all grew up healthy and strong. The pet food industry was in its infancy at that time. Besides, none of us could afford to buy pet food.

Penny and her kittens grew tired of oatmeal at their home; it would stand untouched in their dishes. Ruth and I didn't eat oatmeal quite as often as our friends, but when we did, Leo got his share, if he was at home. He seldom ate it. However, he'd go down to the other house and polish off the oatmeal left untouched by Penny and their kittens. Perhaps this was a sacrifice he made for his children. When those dishes were licked clean, Penny and her kittens were given something fresh, different and, quite likely, more tasty to them.

Penny was never spayed. She had one litter of kittens a year and they were always orange-yellow tabbies—except once. That was the year Sec, who had taken over fathering duties after his father Leo was killed, and who was the last of our unneutered cats, disappeared and never returned.

When she came in season that spring, there were no orange-yellow toms visiting the area. She resisted the advances of other toms through several heats. Then, we always concluded, she was finally raped. It was autumn before she produced kittens, and there wasn't an orange-yellow in the litter. She refused to accept them.

After that one time, Penny always saw to it that the father of her kittens was orange-yellow, probably one of Leo's or Sec's progeny. Never again was there an exception.

If no ginger tomcat showed up when she came in heat, she simply disappeared. Sometimes she was gone for a week or longer. Many times her people feared that something terrible had happened to her. But apparently she had traveled, God only knows how far, until she found an orange-yellow mate.

Perhaps cats are color-blind. Or maybe Penny, like the human animal, searched for a father figure—or in this case, a brother figure, a son figure too, if you will—when she selected a husband.

Few cats limit their offspring to one litter a year and keep the quality as high as Penny did. Her people never had any trouble finding relatively good homes for her kittens. In fact, we took three more of her kittens over the years. When her people finally sold their property in Putnam County and moved to Upstate New York, she was thirteen years old and still having orange-yellow kittens.

Granted, it's fun to observe the family life of unneutered cats. Yet, it is far too easy through thoughtlessness or carelessness to contribute to the horrifying crime of overpopulation.

The people at Pet Pride, Inc., a nonprofit humane

organization, state that "Twenty million unwanted and homeless cats are born across the United States annually. During the peak of the kitten season, ranging from late April to early September, city pounds and shelters euthanize unclaimed and abandoned cats and kittens at the rate of approximately *one per minute.*

"Those who meet their end quickly and systematically are the lucky ones. Countless thousands of others are rounded up and sold to laboratories where death is slow and agonizing. Still others are left to wander the city streets at the mercy of the elements—easy prey for larger animals, easy targets for automobiles, easy marks for cruel pranksters and fanatics.

"If they are quick-witted enough to survive, the cats who range loose in town or country soon attain maturity and bring forth at least five or six offspring (the majority of which are female) to further propagate this vicious cycle."

I know that here in Sonoma County, California, where we live, three thousand unwanted cats and kittens are sent to our modern Dachau every month.

Unaltered male cats are impossible in a city apartment. They will spray the furniture and sometimes even their people, and the best of air-fresheners can't erase the smell. Unspayed females are noisy and violent in heat if they are confined, especially the Siamese.

In suburban areas, unneutered cats are subjected to a terrible life. Toms roam and fight, claw and injure and infect each other. They spray neighbors' cars, porches and flower beds. They get killed and maimed by cars and dogs and people.

Unspayed females produce litter after litter, and often the kittens are given away to unsuitable homes where children may maul and mistreat them. Or they are dumped on some back-country road to fend for themselves. If they manage to survive, and a cat is a hardy, tenacious animal, they go on producing more cats.

Farmers keep cats to control the rodent population. Yet, no place does a cat traditionally receive worse treatment than in rural areas.

Years ago, young farm boys used to neuter tomcats for kicks. Perhaps they still do. Such castration was sort of a symbolic thing. It was a furthering of the prevalent religious beliefs by mothers against all maleness. The operation was invariably performed upon a full-grown tomcat. Afterwards, he became fat and sluggish.

So the myth grew that, if you neuter a male cat, he becomes fat and lazy and won't hunt. We've found this just isn't so.

The spaying of female cats required professional skill and knowledge and couldn't be done by young bucks in barn or garage. Besides, the farmers had a myth about the female cat; she would hunt only when she had a litter of kittens to feed. So they always chose unspayed female cats, and the more kittens they produced, the better. When the farm got overrun with cats, a cat-shoot was organized to get rid of the surplus. Great sport!

Another myth of the farmer, and a lot of other people too, is that if you feed a cat, either sex, it won't hunt. Oh, give it a little milk perhaps, but "a cat only hunts when it's hungry."

Of course, this results in undernourished, lightweight, half-starved cats who are unable to cope with anything larger than a mouse or a young bird. In their frantic state of hunger, they make their strike before the time is right and very often miss. So they steal any food they can get—eggs, baby chicks, song birds. And this doesn't help the image of *Felis domestica*.

An anthropomorphic argument against neutering has been that it will deprive the animal of its rightful pleasure. The fallacy here is the assumption that nonhuman animals get pleasure out of sex. If you have ever watched cats mating or dogs mating, no doubt the idea of pleasure crosses your mind. But what you observe is a drive fueled and directed by their hormone production.

Only the human animal has evolved to a point where recognizable pleasure is experienced from sex. And there are some human animals who will categorically state that they get no pleasure out of sex.

The best time to have the male cat neutered is when it is between eight and ten months old. This gives the urinary tract time to develop fully and prevents urinary problems when the cat grows older.

Castration is a relatively simple operation, which I have seen evolve from no anesthetic to the use of one of the hallucinogenic drugs. With no anesthetic, the tomcat was usually rolled quickly in a large turkish towel with just his tail and genitals exposed. A good vet could complete the operation in a matter of seconds. It was all over so quickly the cat barely had time to recover from the indignity of being rolled in the towel. The morning after, he was a little stiff and pinched in the rear end, but after a little exercise he gave the impression that nothing had happened.

With the hallucinogenic drugs, I've known cats to have "bad trips." Unless they are kept in the house after they are brought home, they can wander away and get into trouble before the drug completely wears off. However, our latest Siamese apparently had a beautiful trip. He was ready to come home in a few hours after the operation, and it was hard to tell that anything had happened to him.

Spaying the female cat requires the opening of the lower abdomen and the removal of both ovaries, both uterine horns and a portion of the uterine body. Usually the animal must stay from two to three days in the hospital, and then you'll have to take her back to have the stitches removed. Sometimes you can do this yourself.

The cost of neutering keeps many people from having the operation performed on their cats. However, if one has a conscience, I think almost any price would be worth it.

Prices vary through the country. In California, castration costs between $12.50 and $25, spaying ranges from $25 to $50. No doubt there are places where the cost is even higher.

A considerable effort is being made today to get local and state governments to establish clinics where people can have their pets neutered for a token fee by a qualified veterinarian.

But if no such convenience exists where you live, it is your duty, and the duty of every person or family, to consider neutering before pets, cats especially, are accepted.

Neutering changes the personality of your cat. Both the males and the females become more docile and friendly. They are better companions in an apartment and much less of a nuisance. In suburban areas, the neutered male does less roaming; what roaming he does is to hunt.

The country is probably the ideal place for the neutered cat, male or female. Cats are born hunters. They have better sight, smell and hearing than any other hunting animal. They are the natural enemies of all rodents. Properly neutered cats, well fed, are big and heavy enough to handle the biggest and toughest rat that comes along. No longer troubled by sex, they will do their job and love it, and be the best and most interesting friends and companions you can ever find.

5

The Working Cat

A healthy cat, neutered at the right age and thus relieved of the demands of sex or feeding families, loves to hunt. That is the cat's job. Ecologically, the cat keeps the rodent population in balance. If you feed yours well, it will hunt for six or eight hours out of the twenty-four—*if* there is anything to hunt.

It took me several years before I wised up to the true role of the cat in a family, especially a family living where the cat has some outdoor freedom. An apartment cat will substitute games it creates for the real work of stalking, pouncing and dispatching. A cat can be quite content with such a life, for adaptability is one of the great characteristics of cats. But where there is hunting to be done, a cat brings a zest to the job that only a person who loves the work he does can really appreciate.

Coupled with the cat's dedication to the hunt are two unusual traits.

A cat likes to bring his people presents. A dog can be trained to retrieve. It will bring you a stick or a ball for you to throw for it to bring back to you again. But a cat, all on its own, will bring you a present. It will lay its catches at your feet. So far as I've been able to discover, the cat is the only animal that will do that sort of thing.

Our youngest Siamese, Mao, before he was old enough to begin serious hunting, used to bring us pretty autumn leaves. Once he brought Ruth a beautiful, flat green stone the size of a half-dollar.

The other trait is the love of praise. Many times, praise is all the reward a cat wants, and the more lavish, the better.

I have often posed the question: "What can praise mean to a cat?" The usual reply is that it means the same to a cat as it does to a human. But isn't that being anthropomorphic, attributing human emotions and feelings to a nonhuman animal?

Yet, it is this trait, this love of praise, that can be used effectively to reinforce the behavior you want in the hunter cat.

When a young cat catches a mouse, it's not mad at the mouse. It may eventually become a tender morsel to eat, but the young cat knows no antipathy toward it. However, let the mouse bite him and raise his ire, and the cat will damned soon dispatch that mouse. I have always administered the *coup de grace* to the unkilled catches of our young cats. I soon learned that each one got the message quickly and took care of the job efficiently after that.

Cats usually play with their dead catches for a while. Some of that play is the tearing-down-the-goalposts sort of thing. But in most instances, it is only a way to break the skin so that they can begin the meal.

I learned the effectiveness of disapproval before I grasped the real value of praise. We were living in our little cottage in the woods in New York State and it was late May or early June, the time for young rabbits to start bursting out of their nests. One evening, Ruth and I were reading when we heard a scream.

It was the cry of a terrified baby rabbit, a sound that chills me. But cats will catch baby rabbits, full-grown ones too, and find them good eating—not unlike humans.

I lay down my book, got the flashlight and went out to the birch grove. There I found our first neutered cat, Leo Tertius, playing with a baby rabbit. Upon my approach, he bit it hard and it screamed. After a little coaxing, he gave it to me. I promptly broke its neck and gave it back to him, saying something like, "I don't care if you catch rabbits, but I wish the hell you'd kill them outright when you do."

He sat down to eat his catch and I went indoors to resume my reading.

Fifteen minutes later, we were startled by another scream. Tersh had gone back to the nest and helped himself to another rabbit. Again I got the flashlight, went out and dispatched this one and told him in greater detail what I thought about a cat that lets his catches scream the way he did.

Thereafter he never again let a young rabbit scream, unless he failed to break its neck on the first strike, which was seldom.

I can't prove he connected the rabbit's scream with my giving it the death blow and him a lecture. No way. Perhaps he just wanted to do his own killing, or he objected to my way of doing it. Maybe he sensed my displeasure at him and hit upon the idea that, by keeping his catches quiet, he wouldn't bring me into the act.

Every new cat that has come to us has had to be taught this same lesson. Sometimes the experience has been harrowing.

The spring Curley, a ginger tabby with a deformed ear, came to live with us here in California, he brought a very small rabbit into the carport. Young rabbits are cute. Curley wasn't a young cat when he came to us—we don't know how old he was—and he hadn't had the benefit of proper catch-dispatching training.

Ruth was in the carport when he brought this bunny in. It hadn't screamed and, indeed, was quite unharmed. She told me later, "He set it down and looked at it benignly, like a proud ma cat at her kitten. Then he looked up at me for approval while the rabbit washed its face."

That scene was more than she could take and she fled, yelling at me to come handle the situation.

By the time I got there from my desk, Tang, our old Siamese, and Si, the young one, had put in their appearances.

Trying to catch or kill a small creature like a rabbit beneath a car isn't easy, especially when you've no stomach for the job, anyhow. I made a pass at the little fellow. A flurry of activity followed, and the rabbit disappeared.

Then I noticed that one of my audience of helpers was gone, too—Si. Curley and Tang began searching the carport, then the adjacent shop, then the patio out back. Then they ducked under the rear fence and took up positions looking down the slope toward a jungle of brush where Si liked to hunt. I returned to my desk.

Si wasn't very hungry when he came in that evening.

Sometimes I've wondered just what would happen if our cats didn't catch rabbits, or we didn't have cats. Keeping the rabbit population in balance is part of a cat's job. I control the cat population in my area reasonably well, and they control the rabbit population. And, to me, their way is less terrible than starvation, disease or poison.

It was a rabbit catch that first made me realize a cat can make a distinction between the size of his kill and the amount of attention or praise that is his due. Our cats were usually satisfied with regular praise for the smaller rodents they caught. If we weren't around to dish out plaudits, they went ahead and ate their catch without our praise.

But one Sunday afternoon I walked down to call on neighbors. Our Siamese, Tang, accompanied me until we got close to their place, and then disappeared into the brush.

For some reason I had occasion to go back up to our place. On the way, I stopped where Tang and I had separated and called him. He didn't come.

When I got up to our house I found a full-grown, dead brush rabbit lying on a section of the newspaper on the family-room floor. Tang was there. So were the other two cats we had at that time, Topsy, another Siamese, and Charles Addams, a black-and-white.

As soon as I entered, Tang went to the rabbit, sniffed it and looked up at me. He had apparently made his kill near where he had left me and that was the reason he hadn't waited for me to return. After I told him what a great hunter he was, he took it to his eating corner and started tearing it apart.

Next to gophers, brush rabbits were Tang's favorite game. But he had resisted eating this one until I had seen it and praised him for it. What's more, neither Topsy nor Charles had tried to preempt his catch while he waited, although both of them loved brush rabbit and eventually shared this one.

Charles Addams was one of the greatest hunter cats we ever lived with. When he made a catch, he brought it home whooping triumphantly by trying to miaow around a mouthful of mouse, rat or some other kind of game.

But he seldom ate any part of what he caught. Having been born a barn cat and elevated to a house cat, he seemed to feel he should only eat canned cat food.

Rabbits were an exception. Even a small rabbit was more that Topsy and Tang could consume, so he'd help them out.

It was Tang who benefited most from Charles' hunting. He knew the whoop of success and could be sound asleep on couch or chair. Then, suddenly, he would be racing through the kitchen to the Flexport, the door we installed the cats could push in and out through, and out to meet the triumphant hunter.

Very often he heard Charles' announcement before either Ruth or I did: that was how we came to learn about it. Once I went to find out why Tang was rushing out of the house, and here came Charles with a mouse, making his weird whoops.

Such homecomings were Charles' greatest moments, and he made the most of them. He'd swagger in and drop his catch. Tang would grab it and hurry away to one of his favorite eating places, usually under the table in the corner of the family room. Charles would fling himself on the floor full-length, almost three feet, and look up for people to pet and praise him.

"Wonderful cat! Great hunter! Mighty hunter! You're the greatest! You're just about the greatest cat in the world!"

He reveled in our praise. After a while, he would get up and go to his dish and expect to be given some food from a can.

There had always been a lot of rivalry between Charles and Tang. We used to say that the black-and-white gave his catches to Tang to propitiate him, or that Tang, as Siamese royalty, was exacting tribute. But that really wasn't so. Charles didn't care who picked up his catches. If no other cat was present, he simply dropped his prize and flung himself on the floor to luxuriate in our praise.

There were times when Tang became so well supplied with game it was a wonder he did any hunting himself. But he did. He made his own catches. He was a good hunter and preferred that kind of food over the tinned stuff. Besides, we praised him when he made a catch we approved of, and he liked praise as much as Charles did.

Sometimes, when Tang was eating one of his own catches, Charles would come in with a whoop of triumph and lay another on the floor. Frequently, several kills were made before we went to bed.

I'm sure we could have discouraged Tang from eating his catches beneath the table in the family room, but I felt it wasn't really too much to put up with. Although it's not too pleasant listening to the crunch of small bones while you drink your morning coffee, a person can get used to it.

When we had company and Tang made a kill, or Charles gave him one of his catches outdoors (Charles never brought his catches into the house when we had guests, even people he knew well), Tang always took the prize to a corner of the utility room to eat it.

He might try to tell me about it in a quiet way while I was at table. I seldom paid any attention to him, concluding that he was teasing for tidbits. Later, I'd find the evidence and realize what he had been fussing about.

On more than one occasion, I've gone to the utility room for another bottle of wine and he has raced ahead of me straight to what was left of a kill, pointing it out to me. I've praised him then, and that was all he wanted.

Most large catches were too much for Tang to eat at once and, unless the other cats helped him out, which they often did, he saved what was left until the next time he was hungry. Whenever he made such a catch, it seemed I was the guy to impress. One morning, Ruth had got up to work on her poetry and he came in with a large, white-bellied rat. She praised him, expecting him to take it to his special corner and eat it.

Instead, he took it to the door into the hallway that led to the bedroom, where I was still asleep. He laid it down, stretched out, folded his paws and waited. An hour later, when I got up, Tang and the rat were there to greet me. I told him he was a mighty hunter, and he took the rat to his eating spot.

One time, when our daughter and her husband were visiting us, Tang caught another large rat early in the morning. Ruth praised him and he saved it to show me. I praised him, but Anne and George hadn't yet got up and he went on saving it. At last Anne came out and she praised him. Then, either because George, her husband, didn't rate as family, or because Tang's hunger was too strong, he proceeded to start eating.

In my beginning days of cat-watching in New York State, I didn't thoroughly realize the importance of praise or use it as reinforcement in training my cats to hunt.

However, our neutered cats grew strong and heavy and would take on the biggest and toughest rats and kill them.

Many mornings, on my way to feed the chickens, I would find partially eaten rats along the path. Very often our fourth Leo would accompany me. His weight ranged from sixteen to twenty pounds. He would be waiting for me and point out the bodies by conspicuously sniffing them. If that didn't seem to get my attention, he would toss what was left of the rat in the air.

That was his way of making sure I knew he had done his job as a working cat. I've never known one of my cats to do this to a kill that wasn't his, unless the

true owner had already made known his proprietor-
ship and had passed on the catch for the other cat to
play with.

Twice, Leo called my attention to dead weasels. I
think it was this that really started me lavishing
praise.

A weasel is a terror to a chicken flock. For its size,
it is one of the most bloodthirsty and ferocious of predators. Weasels have even been reported to attack humans, which may or may not be a myth. For a cat to
kill one is a feat that gets my respect.

But cats and their hunting can sometimes produce
hilarious situations. We brought this same Leo and his
younger half-brother Timmy, also a ginger tabby, to
California with us. It wasn't until February of the year
following our move that we attracted enough rodents to
give our cats much to do.

One morning, just after we got up, Timmy brought
a mouse into the kitchen. Ruth had already fed Leo
Four. He was fourteen years old and weighted close to
twenty pounds. He didn't believe in putting extra
stress on his body while he ate, so he lay on his wide,
hair-woolly brisket with his head in his food dish.

Perhaps, because it was our practice to take lizards away from Timmy when he caught them, he had
brought this mouse in still alive as if to make sure he
had caught something we would approve of.

It started dashing around the kitchen, trying to get
out or find cover. "Kill it, Timmy!" I said and slipped
off a sandal to take a whack at it myself if I got a
chance. After a pass and a miss, the mouse ducked
under Leo.

The chase came to a full stop. Ruth, Anne, who was
just a youngster at that time, and I stood and stared as
if the mouse had evaporated. Timmy must have been
even more baffled by the situation than we were.

Leo went right on eating. As we watched, a ripple ran down his back. Then his woolly sides began to twitch. He looked a little like a person with an ant in his pants. We began to laugh.

Without missing a bite, Leo raised up and exposed the mouse. It made another dash. Timmy hooked it this time and disappeared outside. Leo settled back down on his paunch and went right on eating. We three humans, our laugh over, sat down to our own breakfast.

Praise can make a good hunter of a cat, but the opposite, mockery, can destroy a hunting spirit. We had our second Siamese, Topsy, spayed and she became a great hunter—until she caught a mole and we drew a wrong conclusion.

One noon, here in California, I happened to glance out the kitchen window. I saw her coming down the ridge to the patio with a large catch in her mouth. She went around the house to the deck, and I saw that she had a mole. I called Ruth and Anne, and we praised her.

To my knowledge, cats never eat moles. I've always assumed that the skin is too tough for them to break so they can get at the flesh.

Anyhow, we let Topsy keep her mole and get all the satisfaction she could out of displaying it. After she tired of that, one of us would dispose of the body. I went about my work as usual. When I returned to the house, the mole was gone.

The following noon, at approximately the same time, Topsy appeared on the deck proudly carrying a large mole. I concluded that she had retrieved yesterday's catch from somewhere and had brought it around to get praised again.

"Topsy, you're an old fraud," I told her. "You can't palm off the same mole on us twice."

We all agreed that she had tried to play a cute

trick on us. We told her so and laughed at her. That afternoon, I buried the mole in the garden.

Two days later, coming up from my study, I got the distinct whiff of a decaying body in a manzanita thicket along the way. Checking it out, I found a large, dead mole, flyblown in the heat.

When I got to the house, I asked Ruth and Anne if they knew anything about the disappearance of the first mole Topsy had brought in. Anne said she'd thrown it down in the manzanitas.

Topsy could have found it there and brought it back for praise, as we had suspected. But she hadn't. She hadn't tried to hoodwink us at all. The second mole had been an honest catch. She had been doubly deserving of the praise she sought.

But our apologies to her for our skepticism were too late. Topsy never caught another mole, mouse or anything after that. She stuck to her job as defender of the home and did a good job of that, but no more hunting for us unappreciative humans.

Cats develop special tastes for game. Tang's was gopher—pocket-gopher, those brown, underground rodents that can raise bloody hell with a garden. The only time a gopher comes to the surface is when he enlarges his burrow. A dog finding an open gopher hole begins digging at once. Any gopher can out-dig a dog, so the results are yards of torn up lawn or garden and no gopher caught. A cat is about the only nonhuman predator who is a successful threat to these vandals.

There are times when gophers become so abundant that cats can't keep their population in balance. That once was the case here, and I had to resort to trapping them.

When I caught a gopher in my trap, I always gave it to Tang. Like his recognition of our black-and-white cat's whoops, announcing a catch, he soon knew my yell, "Tang, Gopher!"

I never had to sound off more than once. Even if he was asleep, he apparently kept one hearing channel open for that sound, and he would come charging to meet me, miaowing loudly.

In a very short time, we had to spell the word "gopher" in his presence or he would start pestering me to produce one for him.

Watching a working cat hunt can oftentimes reveal much more than just perfect poise, speed and precision. Once I watched Tang put on a stalking performance that showed an ability to reason and learn.

The patio of our house in California is a triangle bordered by a cement walk. One side runs along the house, a second side merges with a concrete slab where we sit and beyond the third side is a row of dwarf fruit trees backed by a wooden fence. The area within this triangle, about six hundred square feet, was covered at this particular time with red cinders.

It was a hot afternoon. Ruth and a friend and I were sitting on the slab. Tang was there, occasionally demanding some attention. Then he went to the edge of the cinder area. He crouched on the slab and stared across to the flowers and grass beneath the fruit trees some twenty-five feet away.

I couldn't detect any movement there, but he apparently could.

Finally, he got up and walked around to the spot he had been watching. There he crouched and waited. Then he made ready to pounce.

When I saw him detour instead of going straight across the cinders, I concluded that they hurt his feet and so he avoided them.

He made his strike, coming down hard with his front feet and beginning to dig furiously. However, whatever he was after got away. He turned back to the cement walk. Then, instead of detouring again, keeping to the smooth concrete, he came directly across the cinders to where we sat.

There was no doubt in my mind at that moment that he hadn't avoided the cinders originally because they hurt his feet. Somewhere, sometime in his life he had learned that the faint noise made by his feet on those cinders might warn a quarry of his approach.

Instinct, coincidence or accident can't possibly explain such action. One time, or maybe a number of times, he had alerted a quarry by the sound his feet made, and he had related, reasoned and learned.

I have watched our young Missy Manx carefully avoid a dry leaf while stalking, apparently because she knows its crackle or rustle might warn what she was creeping up on. This is such a fine point in the art of hunting that it seems to me to emphasize the cat's fantastic ability to learn.

There is no doubt that the properly neutered cat makes a wonderful working cat. He or she become dedicated hunters *if* there is anything to hunt.

But that *if* can be a problem. When rodents are all but eliminated in a cat's territory, it will venture farther afield looking for game. It is then that a cat can run into danger and tragedy.

Our first neutered cat, Tersh, ran out of rodents to hunt on home territory. Mice had moved into the stone lining of a neighbor's well. A youngster left the safety screen off the top and Tersh, after those mice, fell into the well and drowned.

Tiki, our first Siamese, cleaned out the rodents around our first California home and was on his way to the better-hunting canyon a quarter of a mile away when car lights blinded him on the narrow back road and the driver ran him down.

Charles Addams, our black-and-white, was hunting in the ravine to the east of us when raccoon hunters and their pack of hounds came roaring through. The dogs treed him. The hunters shot him down to show their dogs that they'd made a mistake.

Our first Missy, a white cat with gray and black tabby patches, was hunting in the brush to the north of us when small boys with a rifle shot her.

The fourth Siamese cat we had, Si, ventured onto a neighbor's place. The neighbor raised chickens. He didn't believe in neutering and had no working cats to take care of the rodents attracted by the chicken feed.

The rodents also attracted snakes, in this instance a rattlesnake. It struck Si on the neck and, before we realized what had happened, the poison progressed too far for him to be saved.

So even neutering can't protect your cat from tragedy. But neutering does make contented, happy working cats that don't contribute to the exploding feline population of today.

6

Cats, Birds and Ecology

The usual reason a bird-lover gives for hating cats is, "They catch birds."

A cat is a predator: it loves to hunt. It is a part of the ecological chain.

And perhaps birds are proof of the cliché about living dangerously, for they seem to like to live around cats.

We have a California neighbor who is a bird-lover. He came from Long Island and laments the West Coast's paucity of birds.

I tell him to get some cats and he'll have birds. We have always had from two to four cats, and also more birds than the neighbor has, the full twelve months of the year.

Of course, we discourage our cats from catching birds. It's not too difficult. In the first place, they are well fed, which lets them be selective in their search for prey. We never praise them for catching birds— well, hardly ever—and we do praise them for catching rodents.

When one of our cats does catch a bird, we coax him or her to give it to us and, more often than not, it flies away a much wiser feathered friend. Sometimes, we even scold our cats for catching birds and tell them they are "bad" and that they won't like all those feathers anyway.

Our cats do catch an occasional bird, thus freeing the bird population of one of the weak, the sick, or the old. Sometimes they bring a quick death to a bird that pesticides have guaranteed a slow and painful end.

And, I must admit, if I could train my cats to catch bluejays, I'd do it. If a bird-lover has ever watched a pair of titmice screaming impotently while a jay ravages their nest of eggs or young, he will understand. The jay is a far greater hazard to other bird life than cats are.

There have been certain lapses in the training of our cats not to catch birds. At our cottage in the woods in New York State, we always knew that spring had arrived when the phoebes began awakening us with their fluttering and interminable screaming beneath the eaves and over the windows.

I don't dislike birds. But any bunch of feathers that insists on calling a raucous "phoebe!" over and over at first light isn't going to get a warm welcome from me.

Leo Secundus had gone at this time, never to come back, and Leo Tertius, Tersh, was our Number One cat. I think the screaming of those phoebes annoyed him as much as it did us. Many times, I watched him sit on the filebox by the end window of the long living room and chitter at those things outside. I suspect they were more than just a tantalizing something programing his reflexes to try and catch. They were a feathered irritant he would have rejoiced in eliminating.

This particular morning, we had been awakened by our menace. We might have been up later than usual the night before, or my insomnia might have lasted longer. Whatever, Ruth and I sat at our breakfast table looking out over the greening area below us with certainly no love for the phoebes that still were fluttering and screaming around the cottage.

I might have growled, "Damned birds." But that, I'm sure, couldn't have meant anything to Tersh. He had finished his breakfast and sat on the filebox like a well-fed broker awaiting the Wall Street commute special.

Ruth and I were having a cigarette over our last cup of coffee before settling down to our morning stint at the typewriters. I didn't hurry to let Tersh out, but when I did, Ruth said, "Go catch that phoebe!"

As he went out the window to the platform at the top of the cat-ladder, I might have added, "Get 'im, Tersh." Then I returned to finish my cigarette and coffee, and to continue whatever conversation we had interrupted.

We probably heard the scuff of Tersh's paws going down the ladder and paid little attention to it.

But not more than five minutes could have passed before we heard "pum, pum, pum" as he came racing back up. The sound of hurry drew our attention to the window. There stood Tersh with a phoebe in his mouth. He froze there an instant to let us see, staring through the glass, golden eyes gleaming. I don't know what he felt, but the look on his orange face fitted any description of triumph you want to come up with. "I got 'im!" Then, as fast as he came up, he turned and raced down again.

I went out to find him, but he had completely disappeared. That didn't make me too unhappy. If I had found him, I would have tried to wheedle the bird from him and let it go if it was still alive or buried it if it was dead.

I'd have said, "Bad Tersh! You know you aren't supposed to catch birds." All of which would have made me feel like a hypocrite and would only have confused him. We'd told him to catch that bird, hadn't we? And he'd done just that.

Anthropomorphism again? I'll admit it's something that would be difficult to check and recheck under laboratory conditions. But scores of cat-watchers must have observed similar incidents, when their cats have acted as if they knew exactly what a conversation was all about and behaved accordingly.

Sometimes, when a cat catches a bird and it's a *fait accompli*, there's nothing to do but make the best of a situation.

After Tersh drowned in the neighbor's well, we got a companion for Leo Quartus. This new cat was another orange-yellow tabby and Leo's younger half-brother. He became Leo Quintus, or Quin. An unfortunate accident cut his life short, but he made one spectacular catch in that brief life. It was a bird.

Summer mornings in New York, I always looked out the front windows to see what the world was like outside. This was a regular thing because sometimes I could watch deer grazing in my alfalfa patch across the drive and below the house.

This particular morning, just as I looked out, I saw Quin take off after a bird. Both disappeared in the raspberry patch on the far side of the field.

It was difficult for me to imagine Quin catching a bird as big as that one had looked to be. Yet, a little later I saw him coming up the path with it in his mouth. I went out on the terrace to meet him. He climbed over the rocks that edged the drive, came up steps to the lawn and up to the terrace and laid it at my feet. It was a young partridge about the size of a Cornish game hen.

Several years before, when I still went along with the idea of hunting, I had shot a partridge and knew that most of the meat is on the breast. I picked up

Quin's catch, peeled the breast from skin and feathers with my hands and gave him what was left, feathers and all. He promptly began to devour it.

I didn't praise him, although I should have, but I didn't really want to encourage him to catch birds, not even game birds.

But that breast, the size of two fists pressed together, made a tasty meal for Ruth and me after she roasted it. And free-lance writers are almost always grateful for unexpected meals.

When we moved to California, we still had Leo Quartus and another half-brother of his, Leo Sextus, or Timmy. For the first twelve months, there wasn't much for our cats to hunt but birds and lizards. The latter were new to them.

These little brown and black reptiles, darting after ants and bugs, were an immediate challenge. Lizards replaced any interest they might have had in birds. They caught them, but each time they'd hold one under a paw and, if one of us happened to be present, they'd look up as if to say, "This is the damnedest mouse I've ever seen." They didn't eat them.

We've always had trouble with our Siamese about that.

Usually Leo and Timmy let the lizard get away before they worried it to death. However, birds were plentiful, and until we had lived here long enough to attract rodents, they were eventually bound to catch some.

The slate-gray California quail with its black head plume was something new to our Eastern-born cats. The following spring, Leo brought one into the house just at dawn and let it go. It was very much alive.

I caught it as it frantically tried to get out a floor-length window and turned it loose outdoors. Leo didn't seem to mind. He was accustomed to my taking birds away from him.

But that summer Timmy killed one. The act would

have passed unnoticed except that the cock, cackling loudly, came straight down the bank back of our house, attracting my attention through the kitchen window. I went out to see the reason for this crazy behavior and found Timmy eating the hen quail right beside the house. I had to drive the cock away to keep him from literally "walking into the jaws of death"; by the time I had discouraged him, Timmy had finished his meal.

That year we began to raise chickens again. Leo and Timmy, living up to the conduct established by the first Leo eighteen years earlier, didn't bother the young chicks. Perhaps, associating the quail with our chicks as something belonging to us, they left the quail alone, too.

I have counted as many as thirty quail eating on the slope in front of my two-room cabin study, and the cats didn't molest them. However, if Timmy heard a covey chuckling and scratching in the woods, he would set off full gallop and leap into its center. This sent the quail rocketing in a flurry of beating wings and loud cackling. Then, with what I felt was a look of triumph, he'd sit back on his haunches and survey the world around.

If his intention had been to catch a quail, he had used very poor hunting technique. But if fun and games were what he'd had in mind, he had got them.

From time to time, the quail will almost disappear from an area. Cats usually get blamed for it.

One season here, the quail seemed to vanish. Yet, in my walks over our brushy acres, I found no telltale circles of slate-gray feathers marking a spot where a kill had been eaten. Such clues can be from such other strike-and-kill predators as hawks and owls, as well as from cats.

But that year, two other predators, a quite different kind, had increased markedly in the area. They were dogs and raccoons. The way these predators destroy the quail is to dig out the hidden nests and eat the eggs and young birds. A pile of brush is a quail's favorite nesting place. A cat forced to live off the land may stalk and kill a quail, but it will never dig into a brush pile to get at the eggs or fledgling birds.

Quail allowed to multiply without the winnowing of the weak and the old by their natural predators—cats, hawks and owls—can become inbred to a point where disease can wipe out an entire flock. Dogs and raccoons never let flocks develop. Cats, hawks and owls keep the flocks strong and healthy.

All of our cats have had one experience or another with bluejays.

One time, an excess of jays began ruining our fruit, often before it had a chance to ripen. I got desperate, borrowed a pellet gun and started shooting them. About the time I had racked up a dozen kills, I realized I was simply creating a vacuum into which more jays were moving from the surrounding territory. I hated shooting them in the first place, so I quit in disgust.

As I brought my last kill up from the orchard, I met Tang on the path. He was a young cat then. I was so thoroughly sick of the whole business that I tossed him the dead bird.

He pounced on it, grabbed it in his mouth and started up the path toward the house and one of his eating spots. Then he stopped and looked around at me, the jay a puff of blue feathers in his black jaws.

I've often wondered what went through his mind. He looked puzzled as if thinking, "He's always taking birds away from me, and now he's giving me one." Then he went on up the path, perhaps mentally shaking his head.

When our young Siamese, Si, caught a young bluejay the first spring he was with us, we tried to get it

away from him, but he took off into the ravine east of
the house.

I think it escaped, but he was a marked cat by the
bluejay clan—a Number One villain. His appearance
thereafter would bring all the jays in the vicinity
screaming around him, driving him to cover beneath
bushes or near one of us.

Meanwhile, Tang, an old cat now, could sit nearby
on the driveway, in full view and exposed, and the jays
paid no attention to him. As Ruth put it, "Tang just sits
there as if he had a halo around his head."

After Si was killed by a rattlesnake, our next Siamese, Mao, caught a bluejay. I was sitting on the deck
when I heard the ruckus begin. When I looked toward
the driveway, I saw Mao streaking for the carport with
a jay in his mouth, and a dozen jays fanning out like a
screaming blue comet's tail after him. I went to try to
rescue the bird, but it was too late.

For some strange reason, the jays didn't seem to
hold a grudge against Mao afterwards. Perhaps it was
because foxes had moved into the area and were making inroads in the jay population and they couldn't di-
vide their enmity that much. Then again, maybe the
jays themselves were aware that the jay population
needed some ecological balancing.

One of the strangest scenes I've ever witnessed between bird and cat took place the following summer.
At that time, we had four cats—Tang, Mao, Missy
Manx and Curley. In our neighborhood, the houses are
almost completely out of sight of each other, hidden
among the trees and at least three hundred yards
apart.

That spring, a neighbor acquired a peacock. We
heard it screaming "help, help" night and day for several weeks. Then, it began moving around the neighborhood, visiting the other places. It was quite tame. It

liked to find a big window and strut up and down in front of it, admiring its reflection.

About seven o'clock one evening, it showed up just below our apartment and cut across the turnaround in the driveway, evidently heading toward a neighbor to the northeast of us who had chickens.

Ruth saw it first and called me. I stood on the stone landing by our front door, and Curley crouched beside me. The peacock began its stately march across the gravel. Ruth went around to the entrance to the carport where she would be closer to it. Tang and Missy Manx joined her. I called down to our tenants for them to come watch it.

It was then I saw Mao coming through the flowers and shrubs of the island in the turnaround, stalking the bird. The peacock seemed completely indifferent to him. He marched along, the tips of his long tail rattling in the gravel, his dark blue head and neck held high, yellow eyes looking haughtily around. Mao approached close. He seemed attracted to the feathers scratching the drive, and then he'd look up at the head and sharp beak just five feet away.

Mao had never had such an audience before, four people and three cats. Ruth at the entrance to the carport kept urging him to "Get 'im, Mao! Get 'im!"

The peacock continued unperturbed. He came to the three-foot bank on the upper side of the drive and prepared to jump to the top of it. As he made that hop, Mao pounced and landed just above where the peacock's tail joined its body. He slid back down the length of the rattling tail feathers to the drive. The peacock looked back at him, perhaps a little superciliously, and then, still without any perturbation, disappeared through the brush in the direction of the neighbor with the chickens.

Why Mao made that pounce baffles me. Ruth thinks it was her urging and his large audience. He came away, perhaps swaggering a little, perhaps with an expression something like, "Well, I tried anyhow."

Tang, in all his long life, seldom killed birds. But one of his run-ins with the feathered community got strange results.

In California, a family of black-and-white woodpeckers with red headbands, *Melaneres formicivorus*, made our power pole out front a rallying point. Sometimes as many as five or six would assemble on the crossbars and screech their Woody Woodpecker cries.

It was enough to drive us up the walls. I didn't know what to do about them. There seemed to be no way to scare them off.

Toward dusk one January evening, we heard a fearful screeching coming from below the house. The sound grew louder as it moved around past the windows, up through the carport and toward the cats' FlexPort. Tang burst in with one of these woodpeckers in his mouth.

I don't know which was the more scared, Tang or the bird. Once inside, he promptly let his catch go. It flew to the front window and tried to get out. There, I was able to catch it. I took it outside and let it fly away.

It wasn't gratitude for my deed, I'm sure, but after that, the woodpeckers moved a half-dozen power poles away to do their assembling and screaming.

Tang has always seemed to like to make a liar of me when it comes to the subject of cats and birds.

On three different occasions, when I've been boasting to friends out in the patio that our cats seldom catch birds, he marched onto the scene with a bird in his mouth, head held high, tail up—the perfect picture of the proud hunter Siamese.

Twice he brought in flickers, which are very large woodpeckers, and once a full-grown quail. Each time I was able, before my friends, to talk him into giving the bird to me, and it promptly flew or scuttled away.

Perhaps he was just helping to prove my point: that on most occasions when our cats catch birds, they are unharmed and fly away.

The orange-yellow tabby with a deformed ear, Curley, who came to live with us a few years back, probably best illustrates the cat-and-bird problem. Before we took him in, we tried to find out if he had a home. I don't think it's right to feed any cat that strays by: it may be somebody's pet.

In this case, we found that he had been abandoned at a place across the highway, perhaps three-quarters of a mile away. New renters had moved into this place in January and found him there. The woman had dogs and she refused to accept this cat that had been left behind by the previous renters.

She told us, "He sleeps on a piece of burlap in the basement and steals food from my animals. You can have him if you want him. He's a great bird-catcher."

So we took him in. We called him Curley because of his ear. We fed him, integrated him with our other cats, had him given shots and neutered. During the five years he's been with us, he has never caught a bird.

When he was forced to live pretty much off the land, he caught and ate anything that might help fill his hungry stomach. Once fed well, he could confine himself to rodents and more worthwhile game.

7

Cats and Snakes

My long association with cats has almost always been in country with one or more species of poisonous snakes. Cats somehow seem able to recognize the venomous kind. I'm not sure how. In most instances, they approach one with caution, aware that it is armed and dangerous.

Where Ruth and I lived in New York, there were both rattlesnakes and copperheads. We never saw any rattlers. We did see copperheads. And I killed several.

In California, there are rattlesnakes. I have killed a dozen or more.

Snakes don't dislike people. Even the poisonous kind won't attack a person unless they are threatened, cornered or injured. Like all unstructured natural life, they are preoccupied with the search for food. The larger species hunt rodents, lizards and frogs. If there is a sufficient supply of such game in an area, a snake will make it his home. If there isn't, it will move on.

I lived for three years in copperhead country before I saw one. At that time, the cats we lived with were the two orange-yellow tabbies, Sec and Tersh.

In late June, Tersh developed a painful swelling on his jaw. He couldn't eat. He spent a lot of time lying in the sun. We considered taking him to the vet, but that was a twenty-mile trip and we put it off. Within a week he recovered and we forgot about it.

Across a stretch of low brush and rock behind that first cottage I built there in the woods, I had put in a wide walkway of stone and covered it with gravel. One noon, when I came along this path, I met Sec pacing back and forth besides one edge, looking very disturbed.

He would look up at me, then over into the rocks edging the walk. Obviously, something there bothered him. I stopped to see what it was. At first I saw nothing. Then I made out a mottled, curved shape just barely visible in a gap between two stones. I could see neither head nor tail. I knew I was seeing a snake, but it was dust-covered and obscure and could have been any of several species we had in the area.

I got a pitchfork, speared it and pulled it up to full view on the path. Had I doubts of its kind before, I had none then. Hurt by the fork tine and terrified, its head turned as copper-bright as a new penny.

Sec kept a wary distance. After I killed it, he never went near it or gave it a tentative poke. He seemed to recognize that this snake was dangerous.

The rest of that summer, he crossed this stretch of path with great caution. Tersh wouldn't use this path at all. If we followed it and he wanted to go with us, he always made a detour up through the birch grove.

All of our cats have played with small nonvenomous snakes. I have seen them carry live grass snakes around by their middles, with the ends curling up on each side of their heads like animated mustaches. And they have teased the larger blacksnakes, gophersnakes and kingsnakes.

After killing the copperhead Sec drew my attention to, I wondered if the swelling earlier on Tersh's jaw might have been from a glancing strike by it. Maybe Tersh, only a little over a year old at the time, hadn't known it was dangerous and had been teasing it. Perhaps he got just enough venom to give him a bad time and teach him the meaning of dangerous snakes.

In some way, this vital survival information seems to have been passed from one cat to another among those we have lived with. But did Tersh warn his older brother? Had Sec understood the source and cause of the swelling on his younger brother's jaw? Or did he know about venomous snakes all along?

After Sec disappeared, we took in Tersh's younger brother, Leo Four, and he demonstrated that he knew about copperheads.

Tersh was always a more serious cat than Leo and a great hunter. But I never saw him do anything that might have been interpreted as the passing on of snake lore to the younger cat. That doesn't mean that he didn't, of course.

One hot summer evening Ruth and some friends and I were sitting on the terrace in front of our cottage. Tersh wasn't around, but Leo was up along the drive a hundred feet or so. His peculiar behavior finally attracted my attention. He was watching something in the grass, as intent as a hunting dog pointing.

I went up to have a look. Hearing my approach, he abandoned his pose and came to meet me. I didn't see anything in the grass. I petted him and returned to our guests. He accompanied me as far as the steps down to the terrace. A few moments later, I saw him back at the same spot. He had resumed his watching.

Again I went to see. This time he was too preoccupied to notice my approach. When I got there, I saw a full-grown copperhead stretched out on the grass within a foot of his nose. The snake lay motionless, alert, on guard.

I didn't know if Leo was aware it was dangerous. I didn't know if he intended to attack it, or just devil it a bit. When I reached under his chest and lifted him out of danger, he exploded as only a cat can. He gave a furious hiss; all four legs were extended stiffly, his claws were unsheathed and the hair stood on end the length of his body. I had startled him, and all his actions were defensive and menacing.

Even after I yelled to Ruth to bring the hoe, put Leo down and killed the snake, he didn't relax. He made no pass at the dead snake, as if he were well aware of the latent danger of a reflexive strike that remained in the head until rigor mortis set in. He apparently knew that life had gone out of the snake, but he also knew enough to leave it alone until all danger had gone out of it, as well.

How did Leo know he had confronted a venomous snake? He, like the other cats, had played with smaller snakes and teased the bigger ones. He had always been something of a clown, but there was no clowning, no nonsense about him in this situation.

Some may argue that a fear of poisonous snakes is instinctive. As I mentioned earlier, "instinct" is a catch-all word, a word to cover ignorance. I can't prove that Tersh had been bitten by a copperhead and learned to fear them the hard way. He might simply have been stung by a yellowjacket. Perhaps all the fear, caution and respect our cats show poisonous snakes is part of their innate defense mechanism.

But if it is instinctive, then not all cats have it.

Tersh's brother, Yehudi—so named because he was full of catgut—still lived with his mother, Penny, and her people when he poked a paw in a stone wall and got a fine shot of copperhead venom. His leg swelled quickly, and he was in great pain. His family rushed him to the vet, and he recovered fast after receiving antitoxin.

So, had Tersh really passed on the venomous snake information to Leo?

We brought Leo and his younger half-brother,

Timmy, with us to California. They demonstrated that
this poisonous snake lore wasn't limited to copperheads. They treated the California rattlesnakes with
the same caution they had the copperheads back East.

There may be a simple explanation. I've heard it
said that a copperhead smells like cucumbers. Perhaps
all poisonous snakes smell like cucumbers. That would
make a transfer of information easy, or easier.

In California, Timmy knew our first three Siamese
cats and could have passed on his snake wisdom to
them. Of course, the Siamese might have met up with
rattlesnakes at one time or another in their forays over
our acres and beyond. But Topsy, our second Siamese,
was the first to show me an awareness of the rattlesnake menace.

One August evening, our daughter Anne dragged
me away from TV, saying that a rattlesnake was buzzing just the other side of the patio fence. With some
skepticism, I went to investigate.

The ridge beyond the patio fence rose abruptly and
was covered with a scraggle of live oak brush that had
grown up around old stumps. Sure enough, a rattler
was in one of these clumps, and not easy to get at in the
dusk. I got a pellet gun, the only weapon I had, and
returned to dispose of this threat.

Right along with me went Topsy, usually a very
easily spooked cat. She moved with determination but
caution. I shot the snake. Although a pellet gun doesn't
make much noise, Topsy was so intent upon the snake
danger that my several shots didn't frighten her.

Anne brought me the rake. Usually the waving of
anything like a long pole would scare Topsy, but not
that night. I hauled out the dead snake and tossed it to
a patch of lawn. When I climbed the fence after it,
Topsy was ahead of me, stalking it on the grass. She
seemed thoroughly aware of the danger it posed but, if
it had moved, I believe she would have attacked.

Cats can and will attack rattlesnakes and get away with it. The Siamese cat of friends who owned a vineyard used to drag in live rattlesnakes by the tail. A cat is much faster than any snake. If a cat is aware of the danger of a poisonous snake, it can worry one until all the threat is gone out of it. Snakes tire easily and quickly.

But why, on this particular evening, had this snake started rattling? That puzzled me. Perhaps it had just shed its skin. July and August are skin-shedding months for snakes, and I've been told that at that time they are blind and apt to be touchy. This one might have bumped its snout into some brush and felt threatened.

It is possible that its buzzing triggered a sense of danger in Topsy's nervous system. Another incident supports such a notion. But, one can ask, where does such a sense of danger come from? A behaviorist will tell you it has to be conditioned to exist. But had Topsy been so conditioned? I had no answer.

At that time, I went down to my study every morning, a small cabin a hundred yards from the house. While I organized my day's work in my mind, I shaved with my electric shaver.

The cats, Timmy and Tiki, our first Siamese, came into my study regularly. They even slept there. But Topsy, more of a house cat, seldom came in; she had never heard my shaver.

Then, for some reason, I had occasion to do my shaving up in the house. I sat in my usual chair in the living room. Topsy was outside when I started. The sound of the shaver brought her in at once and straight toward me, stalking.

My first thought was that she was frightened. But if that had really been the case, she would simply have disappeared.

No. She was definitely not frightened. She approached me cautiously, stealthily, her blue eyes alert, her whole body tense, keyed for sudden action. I felt that she was prepared to attack. But to attack what? She came to within three or four feet of where I sat. I talked to her soothingly and went on shaving. When I finished, she backed away and left the living room.

My conclusion: she connected the sound of my shaver with the buzzing of a rattler. She appeared the next morning when I shaved, again cautiously. But, after several mornings, she seemed to realize that this buzzing was not a snake threatening her territory, or maybe me.

Then there was the instance of our young Siamese, Si. We had lived in our second house in California for ten years and I never encountered a rattlesnake near it. However, one night about eleven o'clock, I heard a snarl at the FlexPort in the utility room. I went to check up and met Si.

He went on through the kitchen and up to the living room with a sort of crawling gait.

At that time, we were plagued by an unneutered tomcat in the neighborhood. He would prowl around our house at night, lie in wait for our cats and jump them if he caught them off guard.

I assumed this had happened and that, in the fracas, Si, a much smaller cat, had been injured. I followed him to a chair he had climbed into and felt him over. He protested a little, but I could find nothing wrong with him.

I expected him to be all right by morning. But he wasn't. If anything, he was worse. I examined him again. There seemed to be a swelling along his neck, but I could find nothing that indicated anything more than teeth or claw marks.

Our vet had told me once that the bite or scratch of a feral cat is highly septic. I felt that explained Si's condition.

But he didn't improve that day. He was worse that night. We had no reason to suspect a snake bite: I hadn't even heard of a rattlesnake in the neighborhood that season. Yet, Si's deteriorating condition indicated something worse than a tomcat scratch or bite.

The next morning I took him to the vet. Even he wasn't positive of a rattlesnake bite, but from his examination that was his conclusion. By then, though, it was too late for serum to help Si. He died later in the day.

We were only able to speculate upon what had happened. Our four cats at that time were all great hunters and had reduced the rodent population around us to almost zero. Si, youngest of the cats, had started ranging farther in search of game. This was July, dangerous rattlesnake season, and Si could have met up with one on a foray. Perhaps the snake had struck him without warning. Perhaps the other cats had not properly briefed him on the dangers of poisonous snakes.

After all, Tang, our fifteen-year-old Siamese at that time, was the only one of our cats whose life went back to Timmy and Topsy and thus was a link in the chain of venomous snake lore. And Tang, to our knowledge, hadn't confronted a rattlesnake in ten years.

More likely, Si's death was the result of an accident or a bit of bad luck on his part, compounded by my misinterpretation of the circumstances. The snarl I had heard at the FlexPort had not been an encounter with a feral tomcat, but was Si's reaction to the pain caused by the pressure of the door's plastic leaves upon his wound.

During snake season, when our cats walk cautiously, watching where they make each step, we exercise caution ourselves. Only two or three times have we found poisonous snakes in the area.

But when cats walk with such caution, snakes have

been there. Snakes don't stay long in one place. They come in search of food. If, as usual, cats have cleaned out the rodents, the snakes' source of food, there's no reason for them to stay.

One evening this past spring, I got a frantic call from a neighbor to come over and kill a rattlesnake. She had two small children and her husband wasn't home from work yet. I killed a thirty-four inch rattler within a couple of yards of their front step.

How had they discovered the snake? Their young female cat had teased it until it started rattling.

The cat was unharmed. As I said before, a cat is faster than any snake—when it knows what it's up against. In this instance, the rattler was undoubtedly just passing through, because the neighborhood cats had left few rodents for it to catch. But had one of the youngsters met up with this snake before the young cat did, the confrontation might have been fatal.

A dog will sometimes bark a warning if a snake is on home territory. But a dog does little about the rodent population, which is the reason the snake will be there.

So, if you live in poisonous snake country, your well-cared-for cat is your best insurance against a run-in with one of them.

8

The Easter Rabbit

Ruth and I lived with cats for ten years before our daughter, Anne, was born in May of 1941.

When anyone asked why we waited so long to start a family, my usual reply was, "We were in the Depression. We were free-lance writers. And any free-lance writers who got a family before they had something pretty good going for them in the writing racket didn't stay free lance very long."

If anyone asked why we decided to start a family when we did, I said, "Most couples get kittens for their kids to play with; we decided to get a baby for our cats to play with." That wasn't true, of course, but it was good for a laugh.

As Ruth progressed in pregnancy, Leo Four, or Leo, and Leo Five, Quin, were disturbed by the increasing bulge that took away her lap. They accepted Anne from the hospital with moderate curiosity, checking out the new smells. That Ruth had a lap again pleased Leo; but when she nursed Anne, he would climb up and try to crowd the warm bundle she held out of the way.

When Anne cried, both cats came to investigate if they were in the house, and Leo, especially, would pace around as if very concerned. Later, when the baby was able to toddle, if she fell and bumped herself and began to cry, Leo would go and rub against her. Possibly he was only disturbed by the loud strange noise she was making and not really trying to console her.

We knew the old wives' tale about cats sitting on sleeping babies and sucking away their breath. It's utter nonsense, but we kept the nursery door closed when Anne was little and asleep. After all, Leo weighed at least eighteen pounds, more than twice her weight.

Like most cats, Leo objected to closed doors—closed doors that are sometimes open. From time to time he would check the closed nursery door with a push. One day it opened. I happened to hear it and tiptoed up to see what would happen.

Leo checked out the room, went to the crib and squeezed between the bars. He sniffed the bed and the sleeping baby, then climbed up on the soft bundle and settled down for a nap.

The soft lump was unsteady and it disturbed him. After a while, his eighteen pounds of furriness began to disturb Anne. With a grunt, she shifted beneath the blankets and rolled him off. He lay a moment on his back, all four legs in the air, while he gave her a slightly indignant look. Then, he seemed to reassess this spot as a place to sleep and curled up beside her.

I went in then and lifted him out, explaining that he was too big to sleep in Anne's bed while she was in it. I don't know if he understood what I said. However, he never tried to sleep with her again until she was much older.

Leo always seemed to treat Anne like another kitten—someone to tolerate, entertain, look after. If she got too rough with her games, or he got tired of being dressed in doll clothing, he just walked off and left her.

After an accident killed Quin, we replaced him

with Leo Sixth, or Timmy. He and Anne played together, romping around the house like two kids, or like
two cats of the same age. A sort of sibling rivalry even
seemed to develop between them. Occasionally, a real
fight would break out.

I recall one such battle on the stairway. Anne, no
more than a toddler, was kicking at Timmy and storm-
ing at him in very indelicate human language. Timmy
was lashing back at her, claws out, screaming at the
top of his lungs in probably very indelicate cat language.

Ruth and I usually sided with Timmy and said
things like, "Anne! Be nice to Timmy, now. You're
bigger than he is, you know. You might hurt him."

At the time, I'm sure they saw the fight as between
equals. I don't think Anne really considered herself
bigger, or that Timmy saw himself as smaller. However, he very quickly realized that big humans were on
his side. At a threat of aggression from Anne, he would
begin screaming, as if yelling, "Hey folks, she's picking
on me again!"

Anne eventually realized she really was bigger
than Timmy, and their quarreling tapered off.

In New York, where this took place, we had a cat
ladder to our bedroom window. At night, we left the
steel casement sash open about four inches so the cats
could go and come as they pleased.

Our bedroom was on two levels, with the beds on
the upper level. The cats had to pass between our beds
and down three steps to the stairway door on a lower
level which was left open just enough for them to get
through. Sometimes, a cat tried to sleep with us, but
we discouraged it. Leo was so heavy that if he slept
outside the covers you couldn't turn over or move. If he
slept under the covers he tried to push you out of bed.

The bedroom opened onto a landing. Across this landing was the door to Anne's room. The stairway went down and turned to the left to a larger landing above three more steps down into the living room. A thirty-inch-high partition with a wide, flat top separated this area from the lower-level living room. Against this partition stood a serving table. Around to the right on this landing level was the kitchen. Straight across from the foot of the stairway, French doors opened into the dining room. The refrigerator stood between these doors and the kitchen.

Our trestle-type dining table, capable of seating eight, stood against one wall of the dining room. At mealtime I sat at the end nearest the kitchen. Around the corner to my right was Anne's chair. Beside her sat Ruth.

Other chairs, shoved under the table, were placed down the side and at the far end. Their curved backs permitted a cat to sit on the seat and have his head above the table edge.

A meal seldom passed—breakfast, lunch or dinner—that Leo didn't occupy one of those chairs, his large, round, orange-yellow face and golden eyes watching all that went on. He wasn't hungry. Apparently he just liked to listen to our conversation.

All this detail is to spell out the exact setting for the Easter rabbit.

That spring, Anne was learning to talk and, as Easter approached, conversation at table turned to the Easter Bunny and the eggs the Easter Bunny was supposed to lay. We were setting her up to search the house Easter morning for the eggs Ruth would color and hide. Leo sat through all these conversations, hearing whatever a cat hears when he listens to people talk.

About four o'clock Easter morning, Ruth's hoarse whisper woke me. "Paul! Wake up! I heard a scream!"

My hand reached for the flashlight by my bed. I heard a thumping on the stairway and froze. Then the house became suddenly silent.

I switched on the flashlight and headed for the bedroom door. It was partly open, as usual, for the cats, and I eased it wider. The landing was empty and I saw nothing on the stairs. Cautiously, I opened Anne's door and beamed the light on her crib. I was relieved to see her sleeping peacefully.

Closing her door quietly, I crept downstairs. There, on the landing by the serving table and the railing, crouched Leo, holding a full-grown rabbit by the back of its neck.

It was like a weird dream. The flashlight showed him with his head turned so he could look up at me and still not lose his grip on the rabbit.

Eagerness, excitement and triumph characterized his expression, in my mind.

At that moment the rabbit kicked, showing that it was very much alive. Leo became preoccupied with keeping his hold on it. I reached down and took the rabbit by the ears and body, squeezing the flashlight between my upper arm and ribs.

Leo released his catch to me without protest.

Relieved that our scare had been over nothing more serious than this, but furious at being awakened at this hour, I said, "Leo, you're an idiot."

I took the rabbit down to the front door, unlocked and fumbled it open and placed the rabbit on the terrace. It promptly bounded away, demonstrating its perfectly good health.

When I returned to the landing, Leo was sniffing over the spot where he had held the rabbit. He had seen me take it. He had let me take it. Yet, he could not seem to understand how it had so completely vanished. He looked up at me now with a vastly different expres-

sion. Disgust may be too strong a word, but he was obviously thoroughly fed up with me.

A cat probably doesn't say to himself, "Where did I go wrong? Why wasn't I able to get my idea across?" More likely, Leo's brain reacted very much like the human brain in such a situation, and he thought, "That damned stupid human. He's too dumb to understand what I was trying to say."

To compound my affront to him, I went back upstairs and said to Ruth, "Leo brought in the Easter Bunny."

"What?" she yelled.

"A full-grown rabbit, and it was very much alive," I explained. "I turned it loose out the front door."

Released from those terrible moments of fear and tension, we now became almost hysterical over the idea that Leo had brought in the Easter Bunny for Anne.

I said, "He was telling the rabbit, 'Lay eggs, damn you!' "

And that set us whooping with laughter again.

Ruth suggested that perhaps he had brought the rabbit in to correct the misinformation we had been giving our child by showing her that rabbits don't lay eggs. That notion made us laugh even more.

All the while, Leo was downstairs where he could hear our fun at his expense. Did he really understand what the whole scene was about? What had he had in mind when he brought in a live rabbit? Or did he have nothing in mind? Was it just a coincidence, an aberration, a fluke?

I don't know. But I just can't shrug it all off in the manner of rat psychologists.

At any rate, it was weeks before Leo forgave us and resumed his seat at the table during meals.

Very often, when I've related this anecdote, I've had the distinct feeling that my audience considers the whole account a fabrication.

Yet, twenty years later we met a woman who told us about her family cat who brought in the Easter Bunny for her kids. (She had never heard our story of Leo and the Easter rabbit.) She and her husband had been talking to their children about the Easter Bunny in the presence of their female cat, and on Easter morning this cat brought in a full-grown, live rabbit.

In this instance, the task was much more difficult than Leo's had been: the cats in her family had no separate entrance, and this cat had to claw open a screendoor while holding the kicking bunny.

For all I know, that Easter morning incident might not have been my last encounter with the same rabbit. I'm not sure, of course. Without close daily contact, one rabbit looks very much like another.

But at dusk one evening two months later, we heard the scream of a young rabbit. I concluded that Leo or Timmy had discovered a nest.

I will never be able to understand why a rabbit will produce a family close to a house with cats.

As usual, I went out to finish off the catch, if Timmy was the catcher, and get the message to him that he should do his killing more quietly. It was Timmy, all right. He was at the edge of a patch of foxgrass that extended back into the birch grove, holding a baby rabbit.

Leo put in an appearance, coming from the direction of the garden, shortly after I got there. The two cats and I formed a sort of triangle. In the center of it, the mother rabbit thumped the ground with her hind feet in a most belligerent manner.

She seemed unafraid of either me or the cats. She hopped first toward one of us, thumping the ground, then another, acting as if she were ready to take us all on. I picked up Timmy, who still held his catch, which by this time he had killed, and called Leo. We with-

drew from the scene to allow the old rabbit to patch up
her family life as best she could, if she so chose.

I had never met a mother rabbit who acted as ag-
gressively as she did. At the time, I had no explanation
for such behavior.

Years later, I came upon this sentence in *The
House Guest*, a book about cats by John D. MacDonald:
"The mother rabbit is the only wild animal in this
country which will make absolutely no attempt to
either defend her young or mislead predators."

It is dangerous to make such a sweeping state-
ment. However, a rabbit has very little to defend its
young with except kicking, and no way to lead off an
attacker except by fleeing.

When I read that generalization, it occurred to me
that this experience of many years before might have
been an exception with a built-in explanation. That
mother rabbit could have been the same bunny Leo
had brought into our house at Easter time. If so, within
her frame of reference was a tremendous happening in
which she had been caught by a cat and carried unharmed into a nearby house, where a human had taken
her and set her free. Mightn't such conditioning have
emboldened her?

Cats and humans, whom she saw every day, had
caught her, carried her and had done her no harm.
Thus she had no good reason to fear cats or men. And
from this experience came the courage to attempt a
defense of her young.

Maybe, instead of threatening us, as I had thought,
she was appealing to us to save her young.

Behavioral scientists are not likely to agree, because such a performance can't be repeated with the
true scientific method, under laboratory conditions.
But the laboratory is a very limited place to learn anything but rudimentary facts about life and living.
Other cat-watchers may have observed similar happen-

ings or, by using the above as a frame of reference, they may be able to interpret new happenings they observe.

Perhaps that still was not the last of our Easter rabbit. As I said earlier, one wild rabbit looks to me like any other wild rabbit. Yet, it could have been the same mother rabbit in September who put on a friendly act, for my benefit, with Timmy.

I was on my way to shut in the chickens one dusk and noticed Timmy on the path. The moment he was sure I saw him, he settled himself with elaborate rear-wiggling for a pounce into a scattering of grass clumps and a layer of new-fallen leaves. And I couldn't miss seeing his quarry, a full-grown rabbit.

Timmy sprang. The rabbit hopped. Timmy landed and looked around at me. The rabbit landed, but instead of racing into the grove, it sat up and looked back at the two of us. Timmy crouched again, making even more of a show of his technique, and pounced again. The rabbit made another leap and sat up.

They repeated this performance a half-dozen times. Then Timmy, as if tiring of his show, turned his back on the rabbit and went with me down to the chicken houses.

Maybe the rabbit knew that, in the open, Timmy couldn't catch it and thus was no threat. Or perhaps there was a truce between them.

At the time, it appeared to me that Timmy had just been putting on an act for my benefit, with a friendly rabbit as his straight man. There was possibly no more in his mind than that—a practice game, a bit of showing off, just a bit of clowning.

Yet, here were a predator and his natural victim playing an innocent game; here were the lion and the lamb lying down together, so to speak, or the farmer scratching the ear of his docile cow while her calf suckled.

Come spring, if Timmy found this old rabbit's nest of young again, he would help himself to as many as luck would let him catch or his stomach would hold. When the lion is hungry, the lamb had better not lie down with it. And the farmer will butcher the calf of the cow whose ear he scratched.

This is the nature of things. That is telling it as it is. That is what ecology is all about.

Perhaps Leo and his Easter Bunny, and the mother rabbit doing the unheard-of thing of trying to defend her young, and Timmy and the old rabbit playing a game were only trying to communicate something to me. It might not be so far-fetched to consider that all living things from time to time, or at all times, are trying to tell us something—if we would only stop and observe and understand.

9

Cat Talk

Nose-sniffing between cats has more than just smell-smell significance, it seems to me.

I've seen a cat that has been fed fish sniff the nose of one who missed out. Immediately, the cat who didn't get in on the fish started demanding his share.

Of course, that's easy to explain. The second cat smelled fish on the first cat's breath.

I often sniff noses with my cats. However, if they communicate anything to me, I don't get it. When I sniffed noses with Tang, a Siamese who lived to be eighteen years and four months, he got a wild gleam in his eyes, made cooing sounds and, unless I ducked, would slap my face hard with a soft paw. I don't know what my sniffing said to him, but it always brought the same definite response. Maybe "Let's play" was the message I gave him.

Many times, I've observed nose-sniffing between cats that seemed to communicate specific conceptual meanings.

Several such incidents involved our first Leo. We were living in New York, in a cottage that stood close to a dirt road only a little way up from the Albany Post

Road. A hundred yards farther along this dirt track, a driveway branched off to a neighbor's house.

The neighbor had a gray tabby tomcat, older by perhaps a year than Leo. His name was Teddy. Almost every day these two would confront each other at this intersection and yowl. Nothing much ever happened.

Then, to keep Leo from catching birds, so we reasoned, we got him a collar with a bell. The next time Teddy and he met, instead of squaring off and hurling imprecations, he charged the older cat and beat him up. They never fought again or even howled at each other. Leo ignored Teddy after that.

The following spring, we moved to the new cottage I had built back in the woods. Our former cottage was occupied by friends, a graduate student and his wife.

In the meantime, we had acquired one of Leo's kittens by his sister Penny and named him Leo Secundus, or Sec. Our friends took Sec's brother and named him Horatio. "There are more things in heaven and earth, Horatio, than are dreamed of in your philosophy." Our friend was an English major.

Horatio resumed the yowling matches with Teddy at the intersection. One morning, Leo came along, going from our cottage to the other one, when such a confrontation was in full cry. He walked between the two quarreling cats and over to Horatio. Father and son sniffed noses. Then Leo went on down the road toward his son's home. Horatio got up and followed him.

I don't know what passed between father and son in the sniffing episode. Ruth and I speculated that Leo had said, "Don't waste your breath on that clown. I beat him up a year ago." At any rate, we never heard Horatio squaring off with Teddy again.

The dirt road ended at our cottage in the woods. Across it was a small field bordered on the east and south by broken-down stone walls.

The front door of our cottage opened upon a ten-foot-wide flagstone terrace, and both doorstep and terrace were thirty inches below the level of the road. I emphasize this difference in levels because of its importance to the cat's-eye view and another nose-sniffing incident.

One afternoon, I saw our graduate friend and Horatio coming along the road. I went out to meet them, and Sec preceded me. Just as they reached the top of the steps down to the terrace, a dog appeared in the lower corner of the field, perhaps a couple hundred yards away. Horatio saw the dog. He fuzzed up and ran down the steps.

Sec, on the terrace, couldn't see the dog. The brothers sniffed noses. Then Sec fuzzed up, looked all around, ran up the steps and looked across the field. By that time, the dog had disappeared over the stone wall into the adjacent field and out of sight.

Horatio had communicated the idea of fear, threat or danger to his brother. Perhaps it was through a change in the chemistry of his breath or the condition of the moisture on his nose. There's no way of knowing if the image of the exact threat or danger, "dog," was conveyed.

Another nose-sniffing incident involved Leo and both of his sons.

The previous spring, we had raised a dozen baby chicks in the house. Leo had been interested in them, but after some early cautioning he never bothered them. By late June of this year, we had chicks old enough to run loose. They liked to scratch in a field of young corn across the drive from the cottage.

One evening, our graduate friend came over. As usual, Horatio came along. He and Sec started to play with the chicks in the field. Their game was to stalk and pounce at a chick and send it peeping in terror. They hadn't caught any but, as the game continued, I could see they were getting more serious.

Then Leo came out of the house by way of the garage. He had been in the kitchen eating his supper,

"tanking up," as we said, for another trip of tomcatting. He stopped on the drive near the cornfield, looked
over toward my friend and me, flirted his tail as if
greeting us and then turned toward his sons at their
game.

Horatio had just chased a chick into the corn and
had come back to the edge of the field. Leo walked to
meet him. They sniffed noses. Then Leo walked over to
where Sec crouched, waiting his turn at the fun. They
sniffed noses. Then the father walked off across the
field on his tour of duty.

Both young cats watched him go. Then they looked
back at the chicks still scratching in the field, and together they came over to the terrace and began wrestling to amuse themselves.

Neither Sec nor Horatio played with baby chicks
after that. We always speculated that Leo had said to
them, "Lay off those birds, kids. They belong to people."

A couple of years before Anne was born, we sold
our cottage and moved to a larger stone house I had
been building during my nonwriting time on the upper
slope of our eight-acre piece of property. At that time,
our cats were Tersh and Leo Four, again just called
Leo, one of Sec's sons.

I had the flu the day we moved, and Ruth and
three friends did the job without me. Ruth walked up
to the new house and carried Tersh. Later, Leo was
given a ride up in the cab of the Ford truck with a load
of furniture.

Tersh settled in and made himself at home, but not
Leo. He ate supper; when Tersh asked to go out, he
went along. Tersh came back later. Leo didn't. In the
morning, Ruth had to go back to the cottage looking for
him and found him up on some boards in the top of the
garage. She coaxed him down and carried him back to
the new house. We hoped that the fact of being carried
this time would make him stay. He spent the day there

and ate and slept but, in the evening, he returned to
the cottage.

When the couple who bought the cottage moved in,
we hoped Leo would get the idea that it was no longer
his home. Not so. He kept right on going down there
and staying in the garage.

Tersh still hunted the fields around the cottage, as
usual, but always came back up to his new home. Then,
one evening, the wife of the new owner told us she saw
him start across the wide path below the cottage just as
Leo came from the other way to spend the night in the
garage. The two cats met, sniffed noses, and Tersh continued on up toward the new house. Leo hesitated, then
turned around and followed him.

Ruth never had to go down there after him again.

Many years later, after we had moved to California, another nose-sniffing scene took place which I felt
really communicated a definite idea. It involved
Timmy and our first two Siamese cats, Tiki and Topsy.

Tiki came to live with us in the fall. The next
summer, we went on a ten-day vacation, and a teenage
neighbor girl looked after the two cats. When we returned, Timmy treated us as usual, almost as if we
hadn't been away.

But Tiki, as we had been told Siamese will do, refused to acknowledge our existence for a week, giving
us the silent treatment for going off and leaving him
the way we had.

That winter, Topsy joined the family. The following August, we took our usual vacation. The same
neighbor girl looked after the three cats.

When we got back, I expected frigid treatment
from both of the Siamese. While I was unpacking the
car and bringing our stuff in through the kitchen, it
happened that the three cats came together in the center of the room for the first time after our return. Ruth

was standing by the kitchen sink and I had just come in the door.

I noticed both Siamese sniffing Timmy's nose. They hadn't seemed to notice either Ruth or me. I had expected that. But when the sniff-talk ended, the two Siamese looked up, from Ruth to me, with new recognition or understanding on their faces.

It always seemed to me that Timmy had said to them, "Look, you dopes! I told you they'd be back. They always come back."

Then he walked over to Ruth, arched his back and rubbed against the calf of her leg before going on to his dishes to see what the food situation was.

Never again did those two Siamese give us the silent treatment when we returned from a vacation.

All three of those cats have been dead many years. We still have Siamese cats, and one of them, Tang, who was with us a very long time, knew both Timmy and Topsy before they died. We have gone on many vacations, from a short two-day holiday to a two-month trip to Europe, and each time we get back, all of our cats, Siamese and nonSiamese, welcome us as if they'd known all along we would return.

The vocal sounds cats make vary. An English professor once assured me that cats make only vowel sounds, never consonant sounds. Another authority has claimed that thirty different vocal sounds have been recorded for the cat. I've also been told that *no* communication is involved when a cat vocalizes—it is just making a noise.

I learned about the "silent miaow" from our first Leo. I thought it was a speech defect. The fine, recent book, *The Silent Miaow* by Paul Gallico and Suzanne Szasz, explores that subject completely.

But the sounds cats make are different for different occasions: the simple miaow of greeting to a person or another cat, the demanding miaow for food or to be let out, the warning cry or scream that means anger are just three. Then there's the purr. Although many people assume it accompanies pleasure, the purr may only express a strong emotional reaction to either plea-sure or pain.

I've known cats who seem to try to imitate or du-plicate human vocal sounds. I don't know if they are aware of what they're doing or not. My old Siamese, Tang, could produce a reasonable version of the word *out* when he came up to my desk and wanted me to let him out on the deck so he wouldn't have to go through the Flexport in the utility room and around the house to that deck.

All Siamese cats are supposed to be great talkers. Our Tiki was no exception. One time he made it quite clear that he resented a certain unintentional injustice and was not about to forget it or forgive it.

Another writer and I were collaborating on how-to-do-it articles, and we had a shop-office-studio com-plex between our two homes here in California. We often used Tiki in pictures, so he knew the shop and studio. (They were also part of his hunting territory.)

At this time, my partner and I had a helper, Ed. A draftsman and a craftsman, Ed modeled in our step-by-step pictures, made drawings, and built parts of projects we were working on. Quite often, he closed up the shop at night.

One night, Tiki didn't come in for his supper or to sleep at bedtime. In the morning, he still hadn't put in an appearance.

A part of every morning I worked in my study, a small cabin I've mentioned before which was possibly a hundred yards between our house and the shop-studio-office complex. From my study window, I could see the back door of the studio.

About nine o'clock that morning, I heard Ed arrive

and open the shop. At once I heard Tiki yelling and screaming. In a little while, I saw the studio door open again, and Tiki shot down the steps. I watched him come down the slope, stopping from time to time to look back at Ed, who was still standing in the doorway. Tiki made a loud, bitter Siamese complaint each time he glanced back.

Then he hurried to a spot beneath a live oak tree, where he relieved himself in a thick layer of leaves. His bitterness seemed to abate a little then, but he was still complaining as he went past the study on his way up to the house and his breakfast.

Later, Ed told me that apparently Tiki had been checking the mouse situation in the shop the previous evening when he had locked up. When Ed opened up that morning, Tiki confronted him, glaring furiously and screaming angrily. He evidently wanted to make it clear that he had restrained himself longer than any cat should be expected to, and that that was no way for a cat to be treated.

Thereafter, when Tiki met Ed—in the shop, studio, office or in our home as a guest—he'd stand in front of him glaring and begin to complain loudly and bitterly. He seemed to be saying that he held Ed responsible for his mistreatment. He wanted all the world to know how he felt, and that he damned well wasn't going to forget it.

I don't know how long he would have held that grudge. But he held it until he was killed by a car several months later.

Tang, who came to live with us after Tiki's death, has always made vocal sounds as if trying to tell us something.

Once, when he and I went out the sliding doors from the living room to the deck, I almost stepped on his front paw. He stopped right there and held it out while he stared up boldly into my face and made vocal sounds as if to say, "Watch it, buster. You came

damned close to treading on my foot." The expression
in his eyes matched such meaning.

The following summer, we let a friend graze his
horse on our half-dozen acres to reduce the fire danger.
Tang knew horses; there had been horses where he
grew up.

One Sunday, while we were at breakfast, he came
up from the barn. Up the ladder to the deck and
through the cat doors he came, talking all the way. We
couldn't make out what was bothering him.

Later, I discovered that before we got up, the horse
owner had come, saddled up and gone for a ride. That
was the first time he'd done that since putting his horse
here to pasture. It occurred to me that Tang had been
hunting down by the barn and the garden when this
had happened. He was upset because he saw someone
take away an animal he assumed belonged to us.

When man and horse returned and Tang witnessed
it, the problem seemed to clear up for him. He never
chattered to us again when our friend went for an
early-morning ride on his horse.

Two years after we moved into our second California house, somewhat higher on the ridge above our
first house, a fire swept the east side of our valley. It
stopped just short of our buildings. Several weeks
later, Tang came in one night while Ruth and I were
reading in front of the fireplace in the family room.

He came to me and talked. I petted him. I offered
him my lap. That wasn't what he wanted. He went to
Ruth and talked to her. She assumed he wanted something to eat.

When she got up to go to the kitchen, he raced
ahead. But he didn't stop at the refrigerator or his
dishes. He galloped into the utility room, stopped at the
corner of the washer and looked back, talking louder
than ever. She followed him and turned on the light.

Facing her through the plastic leaves of the Flex-

Port was a large, gray-brown nose and a pair of bulging, glazed eyes. She called me to come.

I went out the back door to see what belonged to that nose. It was a full-grown jackrabbit, at least thirty inches long. Tang had been able to drag it through the FlexPort as far as its ears. Then he had come to us, asking for help.

I don't know if Tang caught it. Our black-and-white cat Charles wasn't around, so he may have. The animal appeared to be emaciated. Food was scarce after the fire, and it might have been so weak that Tang was able to bring it down. Perhaps it had ventured up to our patio, where our watering had revived some vegetation beneath the fruit trees.

After we exclaimed loudly over his catch, Tang was satisfied to feast on it in the shop and not in the house, where he much preferred to eat his kills.

Another time, shortly after lunch, Tang came in talking loudly. Ruth was reading on the couch in the family room. He jumped into her lap, continuing to make excited sounds. As soon as he got her attention, he looked up through the living room to the windows facing the deck. There stood the neighbor's goat, calmly munching the flowers in her windowboxes.

Whenever Tang came to me all excited and looked at me with wide blue eyes and talked and talked, I made an effort to understand what he was trying to say. Sometimes he wanted me to come see something. Sometimes he needed help—a mouse had escaped and he needed me to shift a box or pile of boards.

At other times, I got the feeling he expected me to turn on the sun when it was cloudy, or build him a fire, or set up the thermostat when he was cold, or stop the rain when he wanted to go hunting or do his privy. I always wished I could explain to him that even a big cat like me couldn't do something like that for him.

When Ruth and I returned from a ten-day trip one time, we found Charles, Topsy and Tang in the house,

each in his or her special afternoon napping spot. The moment we walked in, all three heads came up and all started miaowing at once. They talked like three kids trying to tell us something. We had never before been greeted that way on a homecoming. Their behavior was so unusual we remarked on it, but there seemed to be no apparent explanation.

A neighbor youth had looked after our cats while we were away. He'd done it before. The cats knew him and liked him. There was food in their dishes, so they weren't hungry.

I forgot their behavior until a week or so later when I happened to drop in on these neighbors and was told what took place the night before we got home. Their son, our catsitter, was a teenager with his own interests. The rest of the family had gone to the movie before he got home that evening. When they returned, close to midnight, they saw lights on at our house.

Their son wasn't home, so the father went up to investigate. The youth was feeding our cats, much later than usual, and he was a mess. He and a friend had been riding a motorcycle, and a motorist had forced them off the road. The bike skidded in the fine crushed rock at the side of the blacktop and both boys, although not badly injured, had cheeks and shoulders scraped raw. Getting fine bits of rock out of his abrasions had made the boy late in feeding the cats.

The next morning, the father came up and fed them. He had never taken care of them before. They knew him, but not as someone to put food in their dishes. Had they been trying to tell us about this difference in routine that afternoon when we got home? I believe they were. But it only happened that once, and it could be so easily brushed aside as a coincidence.

Another time, Tang communicated most expressively, I thought, with silence and an intent, questioning look.

Ruth came out to the family room one morning to find two dead, brown barn bats lying on the floor near the dining table.

Tang sat guarding them. (How he managed to catch them we couldn't even guess.) His glance shifted from her face to the little creatures and back again several times. He didn't seem to be seeking praise or expecting any.

Rather, his expression was questioning and worried. Were these mice that flew or birds with fur? Would he be called "bad" for killing birds? Or would he be praised for catching mice?

Ruth didn't know how to explain it to him.

The bats were still there when I got up. Their half-furled membranous wings partially hid the little furry bodies. Tiny hooks on the fore-edge of each wing, used for hanging from twigs during daylight hours when it slept, curved just above each closed eye like false eyebrows. A thin grin of sharp little teeth showed in their small flat faces. Little, fox-like ears splayed from dark brown foreheads as if they were still alert to some thin thread of sound.

Tang offered me the same silent, questioning look he had given Ruth. I didn't praise him or scold him. I couldn't answer him, either. Bats can be good little creatures to have around.

Perhaps Tang, with his definite sense of humor, gloated to himself at having stumped us humans for once.

Such are instances of cats communicating I have observed over the years. I wonder how many such occurrences of maybe even greater significance I have missed. And I wonder how many other people with cats have observed behavior that can only be explained as "cat talk."

10

My Model Cats

You might think that the most a camera could mean to a cat would be a black object a human held, made click, and was sometimes accompanied by a flash of light. I find it difficult to believe that a cat can come to know its picture is being taken.

Cats do *see* pictures. Some of ours have watched TV. Curley showed a fascination for the girl in an ad whose legs turned bright red in our color set.

We have a book about cats that has the head and forequarters of a Siamese pictured in black and white on the dust jacket. A friend of ours had been looking at it and had left it propped against the base of the lamp on an end table. Mao spotted it from the floor and stalked it, tail fuzzed, until he got up to it and could sniff the nose.

When I've shown my cats enlarged prints of pictures I've taken of them, they show little interest. Their attitude is more like, "So what else is new?"

Our fourth Leo was a natural ham. All a person had to do was get out a camera and he seemed to show up at once, ready to be in the picture. I had no trouble getting him to pose when Bob Leavitt photographed our stone house in New York for *This Week* magazine.

After we moved to California, taking Leo Four and Timmy with us, I began writing how-to and do-it-yourself stories for national magazines. I used both cats as models in the photos I took to illustrate my early articles. When Tiki, our first Siamese, grew up, I used him.

But Tiki had a problem. He was cross-eyed and light, either artificial or sunlight, made him squint. When I wanted to take his picture, I had to get everything set up—lights, camera, props and human model, if I was going to use one—and then move him into place and take the picture fast. In sunlight, I had to keep him in the shade until I was ready to shoot. With flash lighting, I learned, he didn't have time to squint.

The kind of article I did most often called for step-by-step photographs of how to build a piece of furniture I had designed for the reader to make himself. The final photograph was of the finished job and usually looked most convincing with a person in it.

When Anne, our daughter, was home, she made an ideal model. But she grew up and went away to school. It took a lot of time and effort to find someone as photogenic, and available, when I needed such a model.

By that time, our cats were two Siamese, Topsy and Tang, and the black-and-white Charles Addams. I used all three in stories at one time or another, but Tang was the only dependable one. When he posed, Topsy would frequently get into the act, but I could never depend on her alone. Charley was inclined to be spooked by the sight of a camera. If I got a picture of him, it had to be fast, and there never was more than one shot.

Tang had appeared in pictures with Anne many times. When she left for the university, I went on using him alone and soon discovered I no longer needed a human model. An editor of a Canadian magazine liked him so much that she wished she could buy all my stories with him in them.

Tang was always willing to cooperate. I never offered him any reward when he posed. He was such a finicky eater that it wouldn't have meant anything to him, anyhow. Besides, it wasn't necessary. He seemed to know exactly what I wanted done. If he didn't, he was willing to learn.

One story had to do with the installation of a prefab fireplace. For the finished shot, I lit a fire and wanted to have Tang relaxing on a rug in front of the fireplace. I set the camera, turned on the floodlights and stretched him out, belly to the fire.

When I started back to the camera, he got up and followed me. I said, "No, no, Tang. I want you stretched out on the rug." I started toward him to reposition him. He backed up and resumed the pose without my touching him. And he held it until I snapped the camera.

Another time, I had finished pictures to take for three different stories. It was afternoon, and Tang was asleep on my desk. I arranged the set for the first project in our family room. Then I went upstairs and got him.

I apologized for disturbing him and carried him down to the set. I placed him in the pose I wanted, snapped the picture, picked him up again, took him back to my desk, put him down and thanked him. He curled up and went back to sleep.

I repeated this routine for the two other finished-furniture shots that afternoon. When I returned him to my desk after the last one, he again resumed his nap position. Then he looked up at me and made a "murping" sound as if to question me. I said, "That's all, Tang. No more pictures today." He then got up, stretched and went outdoors.

Another time he did more than just model. He got me out of a real bind with a story.

One of the mechanics' magazines had a regular two-page feature with cartoon drawings showing how to make some gadget for the home. All that was required for such a story was a script describing the series of illustrations; the magazine's artist did the successive frames to fit the story.

That summer, we visited friends in a town twenty miles away. They had two dogs and a kitten. Our friend had fastened a 2″ × 3″ square of quarter-inch plywood at an angle out from the frame of their screen door at dog-nose height. In two days he taught his dogs to put their noses behind the square board, flip open the door and scoot into the house.

Their kitten was only four months old and too small, our friends thought, to use this gadget. But they didn't reckon with cat intelligence. Quite on his own, the kitten worked out his own method of manipulation. He would jump up and hang by his front feet to the top of this piece of plywood, then swing his body under until his hind feet hit the door jamb. Then he would give a shove, which pushed the screen door open. Flipping over and landing on his feet, he scooted into the house before the door could catch him. It was a marvelous trick to watch.

Afterwards, it struck me that this gadget would make a good story for the cartoon spread in that magazine. I thought of sending the magazine a letter of inquiry but reasoned that I should get a photograph or two of the gadget to send, too. I told myself that the next time I had occasion to go over to this town, I'd take camera and lights, stop at our friends' place and snap a couple of pictures.

But this was a marginal story, not worth a special trip, so I let it slide and worked on more promising articles. Winter came and I still hadn't managed to get back and take the pictures.

Then, one morning, I dashed off a script for this cartoon feature and sent it in. Knowing that most dogs could learn to flip a screen door open with their noses, but that probably not all cats could prove as acrobatic as our friends' kitten, I left out the details of the kitten's trick and just mentioned that the gadget could also be operated by cats.

I mailed the story and forgot about it.

One Sunday afternoon a couple of weeks later, these friends dropped in on us. They sadly reported that the night before their cat had been hit by a car and badly injured. It was in critical condition. I realized that my chance for pictures of it opening the screen door was gone, at least for many weeks.

In the mail the next day I got an acceptance of my script for the cartoon feature. The letter from the editor said that, in this instance, they would like to break their usual practice; along with the cartoons, they would like a page of photographs of the dogs and cat using the trick door.

That put me really up the creek. I could get pictures of the dogs using the gadget, but I couldn't get any of the cat. What could I do? Explain the situation to the magazine? Maybe they'd take just the script and skip the page photos for which I would have been paid. Maybe they'd scrub the whole thing, and all my efforts would be wasted.

After a sleepless night, I decided to set up the gadget on my own screen door. I could borrow a neighbor's dog and fake the dog scene. The problem was still the cat.

Our cats go and come through their own FlexPort, and this trick way of getting into the house would seem ridiculous to them. Besides, Tang was far too big to go through any such gyrations as had the kitten of our friends.

I put the device on our screen door and let Tang get used to it. I set up camera and lights and demonstrated how he was to pose, wrestling the door open. Amazingly, he did the job beautifully. He seemed to understand what I wanted of him.

And, when I developed the pictures, I became aware for the first time that Topsy had been poised at the edge of the print, making a very believable picture of a second cat waiting for the first one to open the door.

Several years after I had stopped doing how-to stories, Tang showed he still knew what cameras and posing were all about.

Two women visited us one afternoon, and Tang put in an appearance, perhaps to get a little attention, perhaps to see if he knew them. The women thought he was beautiful. Of course, I began boasting about what a great model he was.

Immediately, one of the women went out to her car for her camera. I set about posing Tang on the rug in front of the fireplace so she could take a picture of him. But he wouldn't stay posed. As soon as I stepped back, he'd walk off the set. It seemed as if he was deliberately trying to make a fool of me. When I argued with him, he'd look at me as if he thought I was out of my mind.

However, he finally remained still long enough for the woman to snap a picture. She used flash. I had used both flash and strobe with Tang. After the flash went off, he looked up, big-eyed, at the woman with the camera. Then he understood, and he posed perfectly for a number of shots.

This same performance was repeated another time, under quite different circumstances.

A local reporter interviewed Ruth for a feature

story. Of course, Tang showed up to be sociable, and the reporter wanted a picture of Ruth and Tang together. I wasn't there, and Ruth tried to pose him. Again, he seemed puzzled and uncooperative, until the reporter took the first flash shot.

After that, he was the old pro again, ready to pose for as many pictures as were wanted.

11

The Proud and Upright Cat

Dr. Konrad Z. Lorenz calls the cat "the proudest and most upright of our domestic animals."

The proudest? Yes. All you have to do is look at a cat with a good home and good people to verify that.

But most *upright*? The second definition of that word in my dictionary says it means "honest, just, honorable." You won't have far to go to find a person who will swear that the cat is the slinkiest, sneakiest, most deceitful and ungrateful of all animals on the face of the earth, and a familiar of witches, too.

However, in my years of living with cats, from one to four at a time, I have found the judgment of Doctor Lorenz to be accurate.

All of our orange-yellow Leos, from the first to the sixth, were honorable cats. Trustworthiness was passed from one to the next, down the line. Here in California, at the good age of sixteen, Leo Four died. That left Timmy, Leo Sextus, alone.

Friends of ours in town who raised Siamese cats offered us kittens on different occasions. I was reluctant to accept one. I had met Siamese cats in New York, and they were noisy and demanding, if not downright mean.

Our friends had jobs and their cats had the run of
the place while they were gone for the day. Those feline
characters climbed on tables willy-nilly, they stole
food, and one day they even pulled all the books off the
bookshelves.

That sounds like the practical joke of a bunch of
juvenile delinquents. It might have been intended to be
one, by these cats. But the possibility of living with a
character from such a background was a bit frighten-
ing, to say the least.

One time, these friends invited Ruth, our daughter
Anne, and myself to dinner. Five places at table had
been set with silver and napkins but no plates.

We had cocktails in the living room, which opened
off the dining area, and their five Siamese cats social-
ized among us. Suddenly the cats disappeared from the
living room. From where I sat I could see the dining
table. Where plates would be eventually, between the
forks and knives, now sat a Siamese cat, each on its
brisket, paws folded, all facing toward the centerpiece
of flowers.

They made a perfect design that looked as funny as
hell. But it wasn't likely to make me feel particularly
eager to accept a kitten from such an environment.

If there had been an orange-yellow tabby kitten
available when Timmy was left alone, we probably
would never have had Siamese cats. But there wasn't
any. So I succumbed to the wishes of Ruth and Anne
that we finally accept a Siamese kitten from our
friends. He was named Tiki.

Perhaps it was his different shape, his chocolate-
taupe color and his crossed blue eyes, but Timmy
didn't take kindly to him. The kitten was bold and as-
sertive but not hostile. He seemed to want to get along.
Although Timmy didn't attack him, he let him know he
wanted no liberties taken, and that even if Siamese
cats might be royalty, they cut no catnip with him.

Ruth let the kitten sleep with her, hoping for gradual reconciliation. Two weeks after he came, we were invited up to Lake Tahoe for Thanksgiving. Rather than leave Tiki alone with Timmy, who would be looked after by a neighbor girl, we took him back to his original home. On our return from the mountains, we stopped to pick him up.

We visited awhile, and our friends told us that their cats had given Tiki a bad time. Although he had been away only a couple of weeks, the others treated him like a stranger. Or maybe they were treating him like one of their kind who had failed to make good out in the world and had been rejected by his new family.

Having no cat-carrier with us, Ruth carried Tiki when we got ready to leave. He curled up quietly in her lap and didn't protest the car ride. Actually, he seemed pleased that we had rescued him, or maybe reclaimed him, proving that he hadn't failed, after all. Perhaps, like young humans coming of age, when a kitten goes out in the world he is expected to make good.

At home again, we were prepared to start all over getting Timmy and Tiki together. But, when Ruth set the kitten down near the older cat, Timmy didn't hiss, growl, or raise a paw. Perhaps being alone had helped Timmy conclude that if companionship called for putting up with a Siamese kitten, he could do it.

So he set about inducting Tiki into the protocol of his home. And the young Siamese fell right in line.

Now, remember that Tiki came from a family of Siamese who were masters of mischief and thievery.

One afternoon the following spring, Ruth called on Tiki's former people. During the visit, she mentioned she had left a leg of lamb on the counter at home.

"Aah," said one of the friends. "Good-bye, leg of lamb."

With complete confidence, Ruth boasted, "It's safe. Our cats don't steal."

That brought hoots of laughter from our friends. They reminded her of Tiki's background.

Ruth offered to bet them that the leg of lamb would be untouched when she got home. They gleefully took her bet. And when she entered our kitchen, the meat was safe on the counter and Timmy and Tiki sat on the floor waiting for their supper.

Our cats go and come as they please through their own door opening. Months later, we came home from a movie to find a roast, left on the counter to cool, lying on the floor partly eaten. Our cats weren't around. It was hard to accept the obvious fact that Timmy and/or Tiki had turned to stealing.

Several nights later, we were awakened by a terrific brawl in the kitchen. When I got there, I found Maltese fur all over the place. Neither Timmy nor Tiki was present, but they came in almost at once, obviously quite pleased with themselves.

I realized then that the theft of the roast had not been by one of our cats, but by a stranger who had learned to manipulate their door. The next time he showed up, Timmy and/or Tiki had caught him in the kitchen and beat hell out of him. He did not return.

Again we were able to leave meat out and feel confident it wouldn't be molested.

In bouncing the stray cat, perhaps Timmy and Tiki had used a team technique. Timmy had never been as healthy as Leo IV, and by the time he was twelve he had begun to lose his teeth. He was no coward, and battling a feral tomcat at the catnip bar had contributed to that loss. By the time Tiki was full-grown, a combat cooperation had developed between him and Timmy.

One morning, I had the opportunity to see how it worked. A neighbor's neutered cat, Blackie, had ventured over to our place. Tiki jumped him. The two chewed and clawed and screamed. Then Blackie broke off the fight.

By that time, Tiki was winded, having spent himself more in the fight than his opponent. And maybe Blackie quit to have getaway reserve. Anyhow, when he broke it off, Timmy was waiting, fresh of wind and sharp of claw, if almost toothless. He chased the interloper back where he belonged.

Such efficient working together requires, I would think, a certain amount of honest cerebration.

At the time Tiki was killed, we still had Timmy and the spayed Siamese, Topsy. She had been introduced to the do's-and-don'ts of our house by both Timmy and Tiki. Then we acquired the black-and-white kitten we called Charles Addams, or Charlie. The following summer, we were given the full-grown, neutered Siamese we called Tang. In August of that year, Timmy died.

Now, Topsy and Charlie both knew that getting up on the counters, especially by the kitchen sink, was verboten. But there were infractions.

Tang was probably the worst offender. He hadn't been with us long enough to have full benefit of Timmy's teaching of the house rules. Besides, he was mature when he came to us.

From time to time, he would get up on the sink counter. Across that end of the kitchen was a narrow window that looked out on the patio and carport. Birds sometimes flew into the glass; once, a robin took to fighting its reflection in it.

If Tang was around when something like that happened, his reflexes promptly got him up there to investigate. If one of us was around when he did it, he got chastised, but chastisements never kept him from repeating the offense.

On the other hand, Topsy and Charlie, both condi-

tioned by Timmy, never climbed up on the counter—or
they never got caught at it.

So, I was surprised one day, when I happened past
outside, to see Charlie with his white feet planted on
the window ledge. He stared right at me, showing no
sign of guilt over his transgression or fear of punishment. In fact, he looked quite satisfied with himself
and smug, maybe even triumphant.

He was always a sober cat, but this time he seemed
to be showing a kind of wry humor. The corners of his
mouth were pulled back as if in a grin. He might have
been thinking, "I'll show that snooty Siamese I ain't
afraid to get up here," or saying to me, "He dared me
to do it."

I shook a finger at him and yelled, "Hey! You!"
When I got inside, he was nowhere to be found.

After we moved to our second house here in California, Tang gave a demonstration of, perhaps, his notion of honor between cats and people.

On Ruth's desk in one corner of the family room
stood a two-drawer filing cabinet. On top of it she
stored a desk lamp.

She usually got up at least an hour earlier than I in
the morning, and one time she came out to find the
lamp knocked off the cabinet and down on her desk.
Tang sat on the floor washing.

She guessed what had happened and berated him
for what he'd done. The lamp wasn't broken, and she
returned it to the top of the file. Tang watched her do
this. The lamp wasn't knocked off again.

Several evenings later, while we were eating
dinner, Tang jumped to the desk chair, to the desk and
to the top of the file, carefully avoiding the lamp. We
didn't care if he slept on the cabinet, so long as he
didn't knock the lamp off.

To prevent this from happening, I got up from the
table, went over and moved the lamp to the desk. I

didn't scold Tang. In fact, I told him it was all right for him to stay up there.

He watched what I did and seemed to listen to what I said. He looked at the lamp, now on the desk, over to Ruth at the dinner table, and back to me, resuming my seat there. Then he jumped down to the desk, the desk chair, and the floor.

During the next few days this performance was repeated several times. He'd get to the top of the cabinet without disturbing the lamp. I'd remove it so that he couldn't knock it off. Then he'd get back down again.

When I did nothing to the lamp, he stayed on the cabinet.

What was he trying to prove?

Ruth felt that he wanted to show us he could sleep up there without knocking the lamp off. When I took the lamp down, he couldn't make his point, so he refused to stay up there.

Perhaps that's too much reasoning for a cat.

Then let's put it on a conditioned-reflex basis. He had knocked the lamp off that first time and got scolded. Now, when I put the lamp down on the table and he saw it there, he felt if he were found on the cabinet with the lamp on the desk, Ruth would blame him for knocking it off again.

No matter how you look at it, his brain was doing something I think we can call thinking.

Perhaps a year later, Topsy developed cancer and had to be put to sleep. Two years after that, raccoon hunters shot Charlie. Now Tang was left alone.

We got a Siamese kitten to keep him company and called it Si. Tang taught him protocol and there were no problems.

A year and a half later, an orange-yellow tabby we named Curley strayed up to our place. After we found he belonged to no one and respected the established cats, we began inviting him into the house. We let him in through the door and not the FlexPort Tang and Si used. We didn't let him sleep in the house.

This gave our two Siamese sanctuary if any conflict developed between them and Curley, who weighed almost twice as much as either of them. His deformed ear seemed to puzzle our Siamese, and they took every opportunity to sniff at it. But the three gradually became integrated enough to eat together at the feeding place beneath the kitchen counter.

Ruth saw to it that Curley respected the Siamese at feeding time. She whacked him, all solid sixteen pounds of him, when he got out of line. And he got out of line quite often because after scrounging for a living—and we don't know how long he'd been forced to do that—he behaved at mealtime as if food was going out of style. But he didn't seem to object to Ruth's disciplining him.

He did have a lot to learn. He was clean in the house, as all cats are when given the opportunity to be clean. But he didn't know he shouldn't steal food. Neither Tang nor Si stole. But with Curley, it seemed as if he didn't realize that people's food didn't belong to him if he could get it. After all, his conditioning had been that any food available was his for the taking.

In time, he began coming through the FlexPort, the same as the Siamese did. One afternoon Ruth put a small piece of steak from the freezer to thaw on the end of the counter. She came in around four o'clock and Curley had helped himself to it. But he had taken it over to the papers where the cats were regularly fed.

She gave him a sound thumping and an explanation that stealing was bad. Oh, very bad! He didn't complain, flee, show resentment or fear of her afterwards.

For a time, we were careful not to leave meat out on the counter. But we never caught Curley up there

again. So we began leaving meat out without fear of
his stealing it.

Perhaps the conduct of the Siamese had begun to
wear off on him. Or maybe he just didn't want to jeo-
pardize his chances in his new home.

After little Si was killed by the rattlesnake, we replaced him with the Siamese kitten we called Mao. The
November following his arrival in the family, a
"stumpy" Manx drifted into our place. She was white
with gray-and-black tabby patches and linx-tufted
ears. She appeared to be about Mao's age. We adopted
her, called her Missy, and the two became great
friends who played together and sometimes slept together.

One of their special sleep spots was a double-width,
upholstered chair in the family room. On it was a large
cushion and two synthetic sweaters, one red, the other
white, put there for their benefit.

After an evening of hunting, they came in to sleep.
The first one in grabbed this sleep spot. The latecomer
had to get up and go through the propitiatory washing-
of-the-other routine before curling up beside the first
occupant. They might sleep that way a long time. But
both had thick coats, and so, very often, when they got
too warm, a quarrel would start to see which one kept
the bed.

One night I watched a demonstration of a cat's
idea of fair play. I was in my chair by the fireplace,
listening to music and only half aware of the young
cats' coming in.

Mao got the sleep spot on the wide chair. When
Missy Manx got up beside him, she dutifully performed the ritual of appeasement to the one with prior
claim. Then, one or the other did something and a
quarrel began. It grew violent. Mao drove Missy Manx

off the chair. She got right back up, full of determination and fight. He drove her off again.

This happened at least three times. Finally, Missy Manx gave up and went over to a red rug at least ten feet away. There she curled up, accepting defeat.

On the chair, Mao sat on his haunches, proud and triumphant. Then he jumped to the floor, turned back to the seat and hooked the red sweater down after him. With one edge between his teeth, his four legs straddling it, he dragged the garment over to the red rug and dropped it in front of Missy Manx. That accomplished, he returned to his place on the chair. And Missy Manx shifted her position on the rug so that her head and shoulders were propped against the sweater.

Nothing anthropomorphic needs to be read into that scene. It was all there in the action.

These cats were not yet a year old. Quite by accident, I had watched the actions of a proud and upright cat. Many times since, I have wondered how much "honest, just and honorable" behavior of my cats I have missed simply because I didn't happen to be watching. I also wonder how much other cat people miss by not watching, or, perhaps, by not having anyone they could tell what they saw who would believe.

12

Cat Liars, Jokers and Grudge-Holders

When Dr. Lorenz asserts that cats don't lie but dogs do, he cites as proof a dog he knew who pretended to limp whenever it wanted sympathy, long after it had recovered from an accident. This ability of the dog to deceive was an indication to him that the dog was of much higher intelligence than the cat.

I have already pointed out that our cream-yellow tabby, Sec, behaved in the same manner as Dr. Lorenz's dog after recovering from his trap injury. Our black-and-white cat, Charles, who suffered an injury to his back as a kitten, would put on a limp for sympathy long after his back was well. And all either Ruth or I had to do to bring on such a limp was to talk about "poor Charles" in his presence.

But the greatest hoodwinker of all the cats I have ever known was Tang. To him belongs this quotation from Sir Walter Scott: "Oh, what a tangled web we weave/ when first we practice to deceive!"

One of Tang's first dissembling performances was a couple of years after he joined our family. At this time I was first to get up in the mornings.

Once, when I came out to the kitchen, I found the second hand of our unglassed electric clock on the floor. The hour and minute hands were in place, but the time was off. My first conclusion was that there had been a power failure in the night. But how that ten-inch sweep second hand could have unwound itself puzzled me.

However, with our daughter, Anne, getting ready to go to high school and Ruth getting ready to go to a substitute-teaching job, there wasn't much time for speculation. I screwed the second hand back on and corrected the time. Then I started water heating for coffee and turned my attention to other chores.

The next morning, the second hand again lay on the floor and the time was two hours off. I began to suspect that what had happened during the night had something to do with a cat.

This electric clock, built into the end of a bookshelf for cookbooks, had been one of my do-it-yourself projects. The clock housing was a box 11″ × 11″ × 11″ at one end of the shelf that hung on the wall above the refrigerator.

Next to the refrigerator stood a table beneath an electric radiant-glass heating panel. Sometimes, when the heat was on in this panel, I had surprised Tang asleep on the table below it. This table was taboo for cats. Topsy and Charlie, the other cats living with us, knew this and respected the off-limits restrictions. But Tang hadn't grown up under the training of Timmy, the last of our New York tabbies, the way the other two had.

When I caught him sleeping there, he got whacked and told that he mustn't do it again. I was well aware that this disciplining didn't stop him, but he didn't get caught after that.

Puzzling over this mystery of the clock hands, I figured that it all must have started with the table. After we went to bed, Tang had gotten up on the table to sleep. Heat wasn't always on in the panel. This time it hadn't been and he, like all Siamese cats, decided to go higher. From the table to the top of the refrigerator took only a hop. But Ruth kept a fruit tray on it, which didn't give a cat room to curl up. Above the refrigerator was the bookshelf and clock.

Up there the air was warmer, and the electric clock motor warmed the top of the box. Besides, that 11″ × 11″ square top was just small enough to be attractive to a cat.

And that, I deduced, was where Tang slept. However, he let his tail hang over on the face side. His tail had interfered with the movement of the hands, holding especially the sweep second hand so that it unwound itself.

This second morning, I replaced the second hand and again reset the clock. But at breakfast I explained my deductions to Ruth and Anne.

Tang was present, as usual, at breakfast time, and I said to him, "Hey, you Siamese cat! If you're going to sleep on that clock, don't let your tail hang over and mess up the time."

I never found the second hand unscrewed or the time off again, at least not without legitimate cause from power failure.

After that, when I came out to the kitchen in the mornings, I always glanced up to see if the clock hands had been disturbed. I knew Tang wouldn't be up there, but I didn't look to see where he was.

My pattern, after the alarm awakened me, was to turn on the heater in the bathroom before going out to the kitchen. One morning, as my hand started to turn the bedroom doorknob, I became aware of three distinct thumps: "thump—thump—thump." This time, when I entered the kitchen, I didn't look up at the clock but down to the floor where Tang sat calmly washing the sleep out of his eyes.

Thereafter, each morning I listened as I turned the

bedroom doorknob for the three thumps: first to the top of the refrigerator, then to the table, then to the floor. No matter how fast I moved, or how quietly, Tang always sat on the kitchen floor washing when I got there. And the hands of the clock were never disturbed.

I even tried going out from the bathroom another way through the living room, hoping to surprise him. No luck.

Many readers may think this shows too much cerebration for a nonhuman animal. But dogs will feign nonchalance, just as Tang sat on the floor washing himself, when they are almost caught in some breach of conduct like sleeping on the living room couch when it's forbidden.

When a cat behaves as Tang did, he's called "sneaky" and "sly." When a dog does it, Dr. Lorenz credits him with superior intelligence.

However, Tang had to go far past mere dissembling. He had to realize that it was his interference with the workings of the clock that had tipped me off to what he had been doing. He corrected that. But to jump down in a hurry and quietly—that he couldn't manage.

The conclusion to the clock caper was even more convincing. One afternoon, when no one else was home, I happened to return to the house just a little past two o'clock. There was Tang, curled up asleep on the top of the clock.

I didn't say anything to him. I went into the other part of the house where I kept my camera equipment, got camera and lights, set them up in the kitchen and took his picture. He shifted his position slightly but stayed up on the clock through the entire proceedings.

After I completed taking the picture, turned off the lights and put everything away, he got down from the clock and never went back again, so far as I know.

There were no more thumps when I came out in the morning, no more casual face-washing in the center of the kitchen floor. Never again did I or anyone else in the family surprise him on the clock.

Once, Tang demonstrated his apparent ability to think and reason right before my eyes.

At bedtime Ruth and I usually have a snack with beer or dry wine. This time, Ruth sat on the couch with her legs stretched out lengthwise on it. The coffee table with the plate of snacks was to her side.

Normally, Tang was allowed to get on this coffee table, even to sleep on it. However, he always got off the moment a snack plate was set down. I don't know how he came by such conduct.

My place at snack time was in a chair by the fireplace. I could see beneath the coffee table to the edge of the rug that came up to the couch. I also could see into the kitchen to the floor by the table.

One of Tang's ways to get attention was to pretend to scratch the rug. None of our other cats did that. But again, they had the benefit of Timmy's training as kittens. When Tang scratched the rug he always got a prompt, "Hey, you!" from one of us.

This particular night, Tang apparently felt he hadn't got his share of cheddar cheese, so he pretended to claw the rug between the coffee table and the couch. Instead of yelling at him, Ruth, who was barefoot, swung her leg down and booted him in the rear with the top of her bare foot. Taken by surprise, he went galloping into the dining part of the kitchen.

We laughed loudly at this joke that had been played on him.

But I could see where he had stopped by the dining table. He spun around and raced back into the living room, right to the exact spot he had threatened to scratch before. He made an elaborate show of repeating the act. But this time, he looked over his shoulder.

Ruth fell for his ploy. Down came her foot to boot him again. Before she could touch him, he turned and grabbed her ankle with all four feet, claws out and jaws wide. He used just enough claws and teeth to get a scream out of her. Then he rolled free and dashed out of the room with his tail up.

I laughed at Ruth and she laughed at herself.

Tang had satisfied his ego. He had turned the trick on the trickster. I can't explain his action except to suggest that it showed a sense of humor and an ability to think and reason quickly.

Tang's sense of fun and humor, and perhaps his bad eyesight, got him into humiliating trouble once.

One evening, a couple of friends were visiting with us in the living room. Tang was in and out as usual. About ten o'clock, the wife, who could see into the kitchen, said, "I see you have a new black and white kitten." The husband, who had the same view, said, "That's no kitten!"

In front of the refrigerator sat a small civet cat, which are common to our area. When this one realized he had become the center of attention, he grew modest and ambled out through the FlexPort, where he'd come in.

Tang was outside at the time. Not long after the stranger departed, we got a whiff of something that wasn't exactly roses. Obviously, the civet cat had been startled and had overreacted.

The cause became apparent in a matter of seconds, when Tang came in. He smelled terrible, his eyes were watering and he was trying to rub his face with his paws. We figured he had pounced the civet cat for a joke. Perhaps he had mistaken it for our black-and-white cat, Charles. At any rate, he learned his mistake the hard way.

Fortunately, civet cat smell isn't as clinging as
skunk. Ruth washed his face and paws in warm water
while I squirted air-freshener around the house. Soon,
Tang was feeling much better.

We laughed at him about his choice of playmates.
He didn't seem to resent our making fun of him. After
all, we weren't to blame for his predicament. Maybe he
understood that he deserved what he got, or maybe his
relief at Ruth's cleaning him up far outweighed his humiliation.

Years later, I had reason to feel that the trick that
civet cat played on Tang had left a grudge so deep that
it took drastic action to exorcise it.

My first inkling of Tang's unforgetting mind was
an incident with a tenant in the apartment below the
deck in our second house. Milan was the tenant's name,
and he liked cats. Tang often lolled on the edge of the
deck and watched what Milan did on the apartment
terrace below.

One evening, Milan started tossing dry cat food up
to him. A pebble-sized bit hit Tang on the nose. Milan
thought it was a joke and laughed. But up where Tang
was, there was no way for him to even the score with
Milan. He got up indignantly and walked away, and he
would have nothing more to do with Milan while he
rented the apartment.

Even years later, when Milan came to visit us,
Tang treated him coolly. He wouldn't go to him, and he
would walk away from his attentions.

So perhaps it was possible he would carry a
grudge against that civet cat for ten years.

We had civet cat visitors from time to time. They
learned to use the cats' FlexPort and came in and ate
the cats' food.

I bought a "Havahart" trap, and whenever a civet

cat became too much of a nuisance, I caught it, took it up to brush country and turned it loose again. I had no trouble with any I caught stinking up the trap, me or the car.

Our female cat, Topsy, came upon one suddenly in the utility room and gave it a loud hiss. It didn't like what she had said and left, dribbling a bit of its aroma.

Another time, the cats indicated that some animal was under the refrigerator. I got the yardstick and poked it underneath, expecting to drive out a mouse or maybe a lizard. Instead, a civet cat scuttled out and ducked into the utility room. I apologized to it for my rough treatment, propped open the rear door, and it left without one scent for punishment.

After catching and relocating one of these little fellows, months would pass before another showed up. I could tell the moment one started coming into the house by the way the cats sat in the family room of an evening, all facing toward the kitchen and their dishes. If a visitor appeared, no cat moved. Perhaps in Tang's brain the desire for revenge upon the civet cat clan seethed, but he remained still, probably more still than the others.

At night, if one of us came out of the bedroom and one of these visitors was in the kitchen, all of the cats gave us a "don't antagonize it" look.

Some of these characters became quite brazen. One got so nonchalant that it sat in the utility room, gnawing a pork chop bone, while Ruth fed the cats an early breakfast. She had to step around it.

Topsy was no longer with us then, but Tang and Charlie ate with only an occasional worried glance in its direction. It left when dawn began to gray the world outside.

Such boldness called for the trap, I decided. The next evening, I set it in the carport, caught the civet

cat and covered the cage with a blanket, expecting to
take it up the canyon in the morning.

After breakfast, I went out to load the trap into the
trunk of the car and found it empty. To this day I'm
unable to figure out how it escaped. Ruth promptly
named this one Houdini. I tried to catch it again, but it
now was trap-wise. We had to resign ourselves to being
stuck with this little pet permanently.

A few nights later the worst happened.

I was sitting by the fireplace, where I could see the
cats' dishes beneath the kitchen sink counter. I could
also observe the passageway into the utility room between the refrigerator and the counter. There was always enough light coming from the family room for me
to see what went on in the kitchen: that was why I sat
in that particular spot.

Behind me, on my left, was a window with glass
coming to within a foot of the floor; floor level at this
side of the house was almost ground level outside. Our
cats liked to promenade past there because they could
look in and see all I could see in the house from where I
sat.

That particular night, I heard a scuffling at the
FlexPort. I jumped up and headed for the kitchen. By
the time I snapped on the lights, my nose warned me of
disaster. I looked behind the washer in the utility room
and saw a pair of furious eyes glaring from a black-
and-white bundle that wasn't Charlie.

I retreated, snapping off the lights, hoping the little guy would get out of there on his own.

Just as I reached my chair in the family room,
Tang suddenly appeared outside the window, peering
in with a most unmistakable gleam of excitement in
his eyes.

Ruth sat on the couch with her back to the window,
and I called her attention to him. We were both sure he

was the cause of the trouble in the utility room. Tang had had another run-in with a civet cat.

Anticipating another cleanup job on this Siamese joker, Ruth began to complain. Meanwhile, waves of civet cat smell began rolling into the family room. I pushed through them to the kitchen sink, got the aerosol air-freshener and tried to erase the stench.

Then I discovered that our visitor was still with us. It had moved across the passageway in front of the washer and now was between the dryer and the refrigerator. In this new spot, at least, it was too cramped to lift its tail again. I was thoroughly irritated with the situation and squirted our visitor full in the face with air-freshener.

As the smell began to dissipate, Tang let us know he was at the front door wanting in. He wasn't about to use any FlexPort now. I let him in, expecting a renewal of the stink and a cat to clean up.

Ruth began to scold him the moment he bounced in. He paid no attention to her but galloped into the family room without the slightest bit of civet odor on him.

I sat down again in my chair and tried to figure out what had taken place. Perhaps Tang had been hiding by a car wheel when the civet cat arrived. The moment it had started through the FlexPort, he may have charged out and goosed it. Even worse, he may have raked its speckled behind with his claws. Then, without stopping, he had raced hell-bent up the short flight of steps to the deck, across it, and back around to the front window for a look at what was happening inside. And that was when I first spotted him.

That is only an attempted reconstruction of what might have happened. Had Tang's encounter with a civet cat ten years earlier been still in his mind? He hadn't evened the score with the one that got him the other time, but tonight he had paid off that long-standing grudge against one of the breed. Who can say? It is my conviction that cats never forget anything. That is a fact of cat psychology. One always has to bear in mind that a cat's brain is much less cluttered with extraneous matters than a human's.

Tang's actions and looks expressed sheer triumph, so wild and exuberant I can't believe I am far wrong in my guess as to what took place, or in the reason for it.

In the morning, our visitor was gone. Whether it was Tang's probable attack or my squirt of air-freshener in its face, I don't know, but apparently it had had enough of us. It never came back. Neither has any more of its kind, although they still live close around us.

So with all cat liars and jokers I am at peace, but wary.

13

Cat-Watchers of the World, Unite

You may doubt that the world is ready for cat-watching. In spite of the careful observation of the behavior of your cats and the equally careful interpreting and reporting of what you have seen, you are likely to be met with disbelief and skepticism. People who don't have cats, and a lot of people who have cats but don't grasp their psychology, are simply not prepared to accept the far-out things cats do.

Many of the stories I have told about my cats have been shrugged off by my listeners. Ten years ago they probably thought, "Oh, he's just too anthropomorphic."

Recently, Dr. Michael W. Fox, in his book, *Understanding Your Cat*, wrote: "It is not anthropomorphic to say that the cat experiences emotions as we do. It is logical to conclude that they do since they have the same brain center for such feelings as we have."

You see, a change *is* taking place in how man perceives his fellow animals.

In the past, when I stated I didn't feel a cat was color-blind and supported my contention by stories of our cats' conspicuously searching out the color red in magazine ads and elsewhere, the psychologists and biologists gave me the tired look of someone dealing with a child. "The color red," they said, "is warmer than other colors. Your cat was searching warmth."

Warmth? Is a dollop of catsup on the kitchen floor warmer than a dollop of applesauce? A cat will sniff the catsup first. (And maybe that will get a facetious, "That's because of the 'cat' in catsup.")

However, Dr. Fox also writes: "Until recently it was thought that cats, like dogs, are color-blind, that they are able to see colors only monochromatically (i.e., varying shades of gray, from black to white). Recent investigations, however, indicate that the cat's retina does possess a few cone cells that are sensitive to blue and green; a third red-sensitive cell type is suspected. Thus cats are not color-blind; they at least have dichromatic vision."

I don't expect the scientific community to rally around, pat me on the back, shake my hand, and say, "We have to admit, man, you were really with-it all along."

I shall continue to quote Dr. Fox: "But within the academic game of science it is all too easy for the researcher to lose himself in an irrelevant problem, in an intellectual mind-game that may give him the prestige of widespread scientific publication. And he may forget how many animals died for him on his ego trip. A man of science must also be a man of conscience and integrity, constantly assessing the purpose and ethics of his work, whether it involves animals or human subjects."

In a sense, what I am suggesting in this chapter can make the cat-watcher a threat to the academic "game" of science. Cat-watchers may come up with observed and documented behavior of their cat associates that will disturb pat assumptions of the "intellectual mind-game" of some researcher on his "ego trip." We may be able to show that the "many animals died for him" in vain, and that what his ego-trip proved could have just as easily been proven by group observations of healthy, happy, nonhuman animals without pain and killing.

Your observations will come under heavy attack from the scientific community, as mine have in the past, because you, like me, have not been properly trained in the scientific method. At first, you will be ignored, as I was for many years. Then, perhaps, we can buck the system to a point that the observed behavior of our cats will be taken seriously.

Even then, we will be faced by condescension and skepticism. And some of these reactions will be justified. I have heard stories about pets even I have found difficult to accept. This might have been because the account seemed so obviously exaggerated, or because it simply did not fit into any of my own frames of reference. And I may have fallen into the same pit as the scientists, rejecting an anecdote as far-fetched, hence unbelievable and without value, because it did not match up with my own experiences.

So, to combat the conditioned reaction of the skeptics and to increase the possibility of acceptance, the cat-watcher should resort to the scientist's terse reporting methods and understate an observed action, rather than take any chance on its not being believed. However, we don't need to forsake simple language for scientific jargon.

A first rule for a cat-watcher should be that your cat is another living being with whom you associate and is fully capable of all the emotions you yourself are capable of. Maybe not to the same depth. But, who knows? If we could really communicate with our cats, we might discover a depth of feeling even greater than our own.

Regardless of the unknown extent of feline emotions, a person living with a cat should always be consciously aware of its existence. Such a relationship isn't just the routine matter of putting food in a dish daily, changing a litterbox when it begins to smell, or letting some second- or third-class houseguest out when it asks to go out. And it is much much more than just keeping a general checkup on its health and welfare.

I feel that a person's relationship with a cat must be a total commitment. When I accept a cat or any other pet, for that matter, into my home, I take full control and responsibility for its life. To the cat I become the Great Cat God upon whom it is completely, or almost completely, dependent. I propose and dispose; I give it love or bring down wrath upon it; I feed it or let it go hungry; I can keep it in at night or put it out among the vicissitudes of darkness at bedtime.

Unless I have some nosy neighbor with a humane society connection, I can mistreat my cat to outrageous lengths and go unpunished. My cat is my prisoner and can do nothing about its condition, or almost nothing.

Unlike most other pets, the cat, when mistreated too often and too much is very likely to "split," feeling it would rather suffer fortune's slings and arrows than put up with any more human guff.

Now, a good mother, human or not, keeps a small channel of her brain open at all times to the condition and circumstance of her young. A conscientious cat-watcher should make an effort to condition such an open channel in his or her brain. It should be open whether you are close to or far away from your cat.

We know that mind vibrations do exist. We know that nonhuman animals often demonstrate precognition or ESP, or something we human animals haven't been able to grasp and interpret fully. Mightn't leaving this little channel open cue us in to a world that is new and exciting?

To begin with, leave this brain channel open while you're shaving, combing your hair, checking the ther-

mostat, making a shopping list, noting the depletion of supplies in the cupboard or whatever else you're busy with around the house. This little part of your attention records that your cat is asleep in its usual chair, is sitting on the window ledge looking out or hasn't yet come in from its morning tour of duty in the yard.

Perhaps you consider calling it to make sure it's home before you go out. Or you pause on your way through the room to see what's holding its attention beyond the window—just a quick look. Are there birds in the garden, or is the neighbor's cat out? If it's asleep, perhaps you pet it lightly as you pass and say, "I'm off to the supermarket, Ginger," or Elvira, or whatever the name of your feline is. "Must get you some more chow. Behave yourself." Or, "Stay out of mischief. I'll be back around eleven."

You don't know if Ginger or Elvira hears what you say, or knows what you say, or is paying the slightest bit of attention. On the other hand, perhaps what you've said has registered in its cortex and does convey some sort of meaning. You don't know that it doesn't.

If our black-and-white cat, Charlie, was asleep in the living room and someone came in the front door, he would take off in panic. When I went out for wood for the fireplace and returned, he'd dash out the moment I opened the door to come in. No matter how sound asleep he might have been, this always happened.

His behavior disturbed me. I have never liked waking anyone, man or cat, from a sound sleep. It was more painful when a being, so awakened, fled in apparent terror.

One evening when the fireplace needed refueling, I got up and said, "Charlie, I'm going out the front door for a piece of wood. Then I'm coming back in the front door with that piece of wood."

Only the flick of an ear indicated that perhaps he

had heard me. I went out, got the log and returned. He didn't budge from his sleep.

Every evening, if he was asleep, I repeated this routine and always got the same result. Then, once, I tried not saying anything to him before I went out. When I returned, he fled as he had before. I tried just making sounds, not definite words, but sounds that might be interpreted as the same words I always used. But when I did this, he'd flee as if I'd said nothing.

Charlie was a timid cat and wouldn't sleep in the house when just anyone was visiting us. But if someone was here he knew sufficiently well enough to brave sleeping in the same house with, I could demonstrate his reaction to my words or my silence. Yet, I had no way of knowing whether or not he understood what I said, or why he behaved the way he did.

I believe that other people who live with cats may have had similar experiences. Wouldn't all such similar manifestations be interesting if they were collected and collated in some computer bank?

What I am suggesting is that you be as aware of the cat in your household as you are of your husband, wife or children. Some people are only barely aware of other members of the family. That happens. But it's not a happy situation. People should be aware of each other and, if you live with a cat, equally aware of it.

Some little incident takes place and a startling new vista is revealed. This is what happens between parents and children when there is awareness. When people-incidents happen, we have a host of psychologists and psychiatrists to offer insight.

With pets, and cats especially, we have veterinarians to answer problems of health. But we are left to puzzle out the strange behavior of our cats, which has nothing to do with their psychology, on our own. Some such happening, small or large, can give an acute observer a peek into feline character, personality or brain-workings.

Of course, should anything like a revelation happen to you, don't rush into print. Try your best to avoid being like the eager parent who transforms the first grunts of her child into a poem.

Make sure that what you observed really happened. Repeat the details in your mind if you haven't time or opportunity to jot them down on paper. Bend over backwards to be scrupulously accurate. Remember that the human mind always has been susceptible to exaggeration and fantasy. Prove to yourself that you are not fantasying your observation.

Once you are confident of your accuracy, you can speculate upon the meaning of what took place. Sometimes you can dismiss it as just an ordinary, amusing incident.

If the solution which comes to mind only adds to the puzzle, just set it aside as another unsolved mystery. It might come about that something in your cat's behavior tomorrow, next week or next month will shed more light on this puzzle.

When awareness of your cat has become conditioned, you will pick up little incidents of its behavior and file them away. These observations, like "bits" in a computer, may team up at some later date, in some moment of idle rumination, to produce a relationship, and you will get a "read-out" of significance.

That's what happened with Leo and the Easter Rabbit, an experience that triggered my speculation upon the behavior of both cats and rabbits twenty years after the incident took place.

Then, perhaps, it is time for you to try out your cat anecdote on someone—spouse, children, friends or other cat people. It may be met with skepticism, doubt, total rejection, acceptance or kidding. It doesn't really matter which, or even if you may get the reputation for being a cat-freak. You will also find that you got a great deal of fun out of your awareness of the cat you live with.

Pet breeders have associations which meet and exchange facts and information of interest to members. Stamp collectors have clubs where stamps and experiences of philatelic interest are exchanged. Many such clubs and associations exist.

Why shouldn't cat-watchers have clubs, associations or simple get-togethers to discuss their lives with the cats in their families?

Probably one of the worst concerns to confront such a group would be the can-you-top-this-story? syndrome. If tongues loosen and imaginations are allowed to run free, the gathering might come up with some interesting "whoppers," but the scientific potential in cat-watching would be nullified.

Cat-watchers, in any exchange of anecdotes, should really strive for as near absolute accuracy as possible. Many observations of cat behavior can be verified, checked and rechecked. This does not limit the subjects to worms, hairballs and ear mites, either.

And even a discussion of ear mites might lead to something fruitful. I examine my cats' ears for mites regularly, yet all three of them will, from time to time, scratch and dig at their ears. My vet always says they have ear mites and regularly prescribes ear-mite medication.

One day, I connected the deep itching in my own ears to the behavior of our cats. At a medical checkup, my doctor assured me I didn't have ear mites. We got a laugh out of that. However, he explained that the sinuses sometimes discharge a fluid into or through the ear canals and that, because of its highly saline composition, this can cause itching.

Were our cats simply having sinus problems and not ear mites at all? On occasion, I have noticed one or another of them sleeping with his or her head propped up. Why? Was this to let the sinus discharge be carried off in the throat instead of the ears?

I have only been able to get my vet to agree that cats *might* have sinus complaints like humans. He continues prescribing ear-mite remedy. Our cats dislike those drops. They do seem to bring some relief, perhaps because the drops are more irritating than the sinus itch. Perhaps after this drastic irritation abates, even the saline solution from the sinuses can be accepted.

This poses a question. Have other cat-watchers noticed their pets batting at their ears when no ear mites could be found? How about checking out such an observation?

The danger of falling for the urge to top another cat-watcher's cat story is very natural: we are conditioned to compete from childhood. However, one-upmanship is not what cat-watching is all about.

On the contrary, we should examine each anecdote, then consider the behavior of our own cats to see if any of their actions complemented, paralleled or reinforced the account of our fellow cat-watchers. In that way, we can gradually build up a body of hard facts of cat behavior from which we can gain insight and understanding.

For instance, others must have used the method I described earlier for keeping our cats from catching birds. This could be checked out by local groups. It, or other methods, could be compared and tested until we might go a long way toward reconciling bird-lovers to our cats.

Other types of behavior and one-of-a-kind incidents rely solely upon the cat-watcher's powers of observation—and luck at being present when each episode happens. This is not something you can set up for a rerun. Such a happening can hardly be expected to repeat itself in one local association. However, if such a happening were reported to statewide or national groups, reinforcing incidents might be discovered. A number of similar anecdotes could thus support exciting new appraisal of our cat friends.

A good example of such an instance is the behavior of our old Siamese, Tang, one night. In the evenings he always slept on the TV. We had a tenant who lived in an apartment beneath the front part of our home. She spent most evenings out with family and friends. Invariably, she came home ten minutes after the eleven o'clock news was over.

At about eleven-twenty or twenty-five, Tang would get off the TV and lie on the kitchen floor facing the utility room and the door to the carport, where she kept her car. We would hear her arrive; the car door would slam. Next we would hear the outside door to her apartment open and close.

A few minutes later, Tang would go out through the FlexPort and, in a few minutes, we would hear him calling at her door, asking to be let in for a visit. This was a regular routine.

One evening, I happened to notice that Tang got off the TV at about ten-thirty and took up his usual position on the kitchen floor. Ten minutes later our tenant came home, parked her car and went down to her quarters. After the customary few minutes elapsed, Tang went down for his visit.

How had he known she was coming home an hour early? Or was his behavior just a fluke, a chance sort of thing?

Until a sizable number of cat-watching organizations exist, there isn't much possibility of accumulating similar interesting anecdotes. But you can start collecting the interesting things your cats do right now.

It won't take a lot of time. Your cat or cats are not likely to perform spectacular things daily. Get a small notebook and put the name of your cat on it (label it "Cats" if you have more than one). Set up the first page for a recording of your cat's next startling or surprising act.

Don't hold your breath, expecting Ginger or Joe to immediately put on a performance that will be earth-shaking. Just put this notebook where it will be available when the event takes place. Keep a pen or pencil nearby. And, if you want to go that far, have a camera loaded with film and flashbulbs also ready and waiting. Then keep that channel of awareness of your cat open and receiving.

Here's an example of how such a notebook might be set up and how a recent performance of our cat Mao would fit into it:

Date: May 12, 1976, 9:15 P.M.

Cat name: Mao.

Breed: Siamese. Male.

Age: 5 yrs.

Act: The door to our guest bathroom was unlatched. He pushed it open, entered, got up on the sink, pulled one of the two handtowel-and-washcloth sets into the bowl and curled up on them for a nap.

I had my Instamatic loaded with film and flashbulb and took his picture.

Now, other cats have pulled towels down into wash basins and have taken naps on them. Other cats probably have been photographed in the act, too. All I had was just a cute incident of cat behavior.

But keep your record open. There may be more to come and a point of real interest may develop.

In my case: June 8 the weather turned hot. Again the guest bathroom door was open. Ruth happened to go in and found the same guest towel and washcloth pulled down into the basin. However, Mao was lying on

the rug. He began complaining bitterly to her and, as
nearly as he could, indicated that the focus of his complaint was the basin. Ruth wasn't sure what his beef
was about, but she put the towel and washcloth back on
the rack with the other set.

Immediately Mao leaped up to the sink, curled up
on the cool porcelain and continued his nap.

Had he been tricked into repeating his previous
act only to discover that the arrangement of towel and
washcloth made the setup too hot? He couldn't correct
his mistake, and had he been saying to Ruth, "How do
you hang those things back up? They're too blasted hot
to sleep on!"

However, that still wasn't the end of it. After relat-
ing this incident a number of times, an interesting angle in it suddenly occurred to me. Both times, Mao had
had a choice between a red set and a gold set. Each
time he had chosen the red set, despite the fact that the
gold-colored set was easier for him to reach.

It was the similar preference for red-colored ob-
jects by my cats over the years that made me feel sure
they were not color-blind, long before the scientists
wised up to that possibility.

Of course, to begin with, you'll find a limited interest in such incidents, except among other catlovers or
in a local cat-watching club—if you can set one up. And
you'll find few places to which you can report such
data.

A recent editorial in *Cats* magazine, by publisher
Raymond D. Smith, was called, "Your Contributions
Wanted." It stated in part: "There are no firm limitations on what *Cats* publishes, so long as it's about fe-
lines. But we do favor factual articles about cats in our
culture—art, literature, history—and about care and
health. Personal experience articles are looked for, but
we think our readers prefer those in which the feline

characters look, think, and act like cats—not miniature humans."

Such a publication might be interested in the behavior of *your* cat. The address is *Cats* Magazine, P. O. Box 4106, Pittsburgh, PA 15202. But don't expect too much.

I don't see *Cats* magazine as a place for the my-cat's-better-than-your-cat sort of story. Rather, it's a place for reports of cat behavior that illustrate intelligence, reasoning ability, sense of humor, ways of communication, ESP or anything else that reveals the depth of feline character. Here, the pooling of data can begin so that cat-watchers and cat-lovers can get the most out of living with their cats.

There are other places that may be interested in serious cat-watchers' observations: *Cat Fancy*, a bimonthly magazine, P. O. Box 4030, San Clemente, CA 92627 and *All Cats* magazine, 15113 Sunset Boulevard, Pacific Palisades, CA 90272, are two.

Then there is Pet Pride, Inc., a nonprofit, humane, educational and charitable organization with the sole purpose of improving the condition of all cats. Pet Pride, Inc. is located at the same address as *All Cats* and its staff, especially, may be interested in taking cat-watching seriously.

None of these places, at the present time, is likely to have data banks available to store the unusual cat behavior you have observed and recorded. But start bombarding them with the exciting results of your cat-watching, and one of them, maybe all of them, may be persuaded to start building such a data bank.

Meanwhile, keep that channel in your brain open to an awareness of the cat you live with. Be ready to notice the far-out things cats are certain to do from time to time if you keep watching. And get to know other cat-watchers around you for a fuller and more exciting life.